Understanding Israel

Malcolm Hedding

Illustrated by
Mark Cerfonteyn

Sovereign World

© Malcolm Hedding

Sovereign World Ltd
PO Box 17
Chichester PO20 6RY
England

ISBN 1 85240 035 8

Typeset by CRB Typesetting Services, Ely, Cambs.

Dedication

This book is dedicated to my wife Cheryl
and to two very special friends,
Ian and Jenny Moore.

Acknowledgements

To Sheila King, Jenny Moore, Mary Elvin, Connie Madsen and Joan McWhirter who all assisted with the typing and editing of the material contained in this book.

and

To Mark Cerfonteyn who was responsible for all the artwork in this publication.

Contents

Preface

Throughout the centuries of Church history, the Church has, by and large, grappled with and come to an adequate understanding of most major theological issues. However, she has never done the same in respect of Israel, which is somewhat strange since she has played such a central role in God's redemptive plan.

Today the modern restoration of Israel has, in a way, caught the Church unawares, leaving the community of God quite unable to face and influence by its priestly ministry, the very real and vital implications that such a restoration raises.

Our unscriptural doctrines of a finished Israel and of a replaced Israel have not only violated the teachings of God's Word but they have, regrettably, also encouraged anti-semitism and have robbed the Church of an ability to hear God and flow with Him in this closing hour of history. In short, failure to understand Israel has left Christ's body on earth unresponsive to one of the greatest prophetic miracles of our day.

There is then an urgent need for Israel to be understood – both in the light of God's eternal Word and in the light of her restoration, miraculous preservation and journey toward her God-given destiny.

If this is not done, much of the Church, albeit unwittingly, will be led into a partnership with the forces of darkness; who are intent, and have been from the beginning of biblical history, on Israel's destruction. Sadly, this is already happening!

The highly complex issues of the Middle East are polarising christians everywhere. Israel has become a point of heated debate and controversy. The Church is now divided over the issue and in the main is turning against her.

There is no doubt that an unsure theological footing concerning Israel will disqualify us from participating in one of the greatest hours of redemptive history. Indeed, if we do not understand Israel we shall probably find ourselves working against such an 'hour' or at least 'out in the cold'!

If then this book will impart a better understanding of Israel to those who read it, it will have accomplished its purpose.

Malcolm Hedding
April 1989

Part One

Foundational

Foreword

Over the years a number of works have surfaced in the Christian church, proclaiming a wide spectrum of messages for and against the restoration of Israel.

Malcolm Hedding's book, *For Zion's Sake*, is a pro-Israel message to the Church in which he sets out what Christians should know God is saying to the churches regarding Israel.

The author has joined the ranks of those in the Church who believe in God's plan to restore Israel as set out in Holy Scripture. They are Christian Zionists.

'Christians persuaded by the Bible, of God's unfailing love for the Jewish people and responding accordingly'.

We pray for Almighty God to open the way for this and similar books to achieve wide circulation in the Christian Church so that the blessings of God promised to those who will bless the seed of Abraham, Isaac and Jacob (Genesis 12:3) will be theirs.

Basil Jacobs
Chairman and founder
Christian Action for Israel, South Africa

May 1986

The flag of Israel, a symbol of her restoration.

Chapter 1

The restoration of Israel

'Therefore behold, days are coming, declares the Lord, when it will no longer be said, as the Lord lives who brought up the sons of Israel out of the land of Egypt, but, as the Lord lives, who brought up the sons of Israel from the land of the north and from all the countries where He had banished them. For I will restore them to their own land which I gave to their fathers ...'
(Jeremiah 16:14–15 NASB)

I once heard Derek Prince say, 'To pass off the restoration of Israel as a political accident is like believing the world is flat!'

William W. Orr stated in 1948: 'There isn't the slightest doubt that the emergence of the nation Israel among the family of nations is the greatest piece of prophetic news that we have had in the 20th century.' Such an event requires closer investigation so as to enable us to understand its significance and implications, especially in view of the fact that a nation twice exiled has returned to the very land of its fathers. Such a thing is without precedent in world history.

The scriptures and restoration

In spite of Israel's sin and rebellion, which in history has resulted in two exiles, the Old Testament prophets have nevertheless predicted restoration and future glory for Israel.

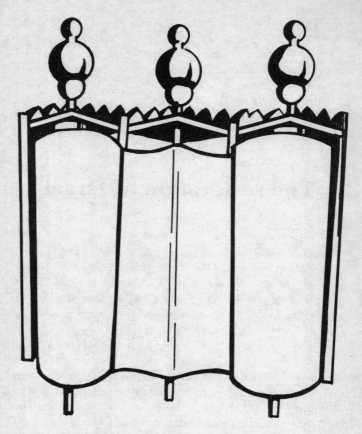

The Hebrew scriptures still speak with prophetic clarity.

Indeed, scriptures in this respect abound and it is hard to understand how certain elements of the believing church can still hold to a 'no future for Israel theology.' This is all the more obvious when one examines the 'until' passages of the New Testament. Dispersion and unbelief are said to transpire 'until' certain key historical events take place. Note: Luke 21:24 and Romans 11:25–26.

The use of the word 'until' naturally implies an ending of dispersion and unbelief and the dawning of a new day of restoration. In his book, 'The Last Word on the Middle

East', Derek Prince writes: 'In Jesus's prediction, (talking of Luke 21:24) however, one key word indicates a limit to the period of Gentile domination — the word 'until'. Jerusalem will indeed be trampled on by the Gentiles, but not forever, only until "the times of the Gentiles are fulfilled ..."'

History has thus seen Israel twice exiled from her land — in 586 BC under Nebuchadnezzar, of Babylon, and in 70 AD under Titus, of Rome. The prophet Isaiah clearly predicted this twofold judgment, but at the same time he spoke of Israel's regathering:

> 'Then it will happen on that day that the Lord will again recover the second time with His hand, the remnant of His people, who will remain, from Assyria, Egypt, Pathros, Cush, Elam, Shinar, Hamath and from the islands of the sea. And He will lift up a standard for the nations, and will assemble the banished ones of Israel, and will gather the dispersed of Judah from the four corners of the earth ...'   (Isaiah 11:11–12 NASB)

It is therefore interesting to note that on almost every occasion when God speaks of exilic judgment He underlines His intention to restore them again to the land and then to Himself.

> '... Fear not, O Jacob My servant,' declares the Lord, 'and do not be dismayed, O Israel; for behold, I will save you from afar, and your offspring from the land of their captivity. And Jacob shall return, and shall be quiet and at ease, and no one shall make him afraid. 'For I am with you,' declares the Lord, 'to save you, for I will destroy completely all the nations where I have scattered you, only I will not destroy you completely but I will chasten you justly, and will by no means leave you unpunished ...'   (Jeremiah 30:10–11 NASB)

We have thus seen this happen on two occasions just as God said it would happen. Indeed the 14th May 1948 saw the nation restored to her land for the second and final time. Never again will she be uprooted.

7

> 'I will plant them on their land, and they will not again be uprooted out from their land which I have given them, says the Lord.'
>
> (Amos 9:15)

Moreover, the prophet Jeremiah talks of a restoration of the walls of Jerusalem that has, as yet, never been fulfilled. Why would the Holy Spirit bother with details like this if they have no real significance? The answer quite simply lies in this: He wants us to have no doubt about Israel's restoration to the land, to Jerusalem and to the Lord.

Thus we can expect this prophesy to be fulfilled in the very near future.

> 'Behold, days are coming,' declares the Lord, 'when the city shall be rebuilt for the Lord from the tower of Hananel to the Corner Gate. And the measuring line shall go out farther straight ahead to the hill Gareb, then it will turn to Goach. And the whole valley of dead bodies and of the ashes, and all the fields as far as the brook Kidron, to the corner of the Horse gate toward the East, shall be holy to the Lord; it shall not be plucked up or overthrown any more forever ...'
>
> (Jeremiah 31:38–40 NASB)

All this quite simply means that God has a future for physical Israel and that her restoration is not a political accident but a divine accomplishment!

Milton B. Lindberg in his book, 'The Jew and Modern Israel', published by Moody Books, writes: 'The context of Jeremiah's prophecy reveals wonderful conditions not yet realised in Jerusalem and its people, but the present correspondence between the prophecy and the city's boundary to the North and West is a gleam of light pointing to a glorious millennial day ...'

Indeed, one prophecy that has been accurately fulfilled only as a result of Israel's physical restoration is that of Zechariah 2:4 which speaks of Jerusalem's populace spilling over the walls.

'... Jerusalem will be inhabited without walls –
Hebrews: like unwalled villages – because of the multitude of men and cattle within it ...'

It must be underlined that the fulfilment of this prophetic
statement was entirely dependent upon a restored Jewish
state for it has no other fulfilment in history.

Again Milton B. Lindberg writes: '... what he prophesied
concerning the building of Jerusalem has no fulfilment until
recent years.'

In bringing this section to a close may I point out that
scripture speaks of Israel's restoration to the land before
restoration to the Lord.

'Behold I will gather them out of all the lands to which I
have driven them in My anger, in My wrath, and in
great indignation; and I will bring them back to this
place and make them dwell in safety. And they shall be
My people, and I will be their God; and I will give them
one heart and one way, that they may fear Me always,
for their own good, and for the good of their children
after them.'   (Jeremiah 32:37–39 NASB)

Ezekiel makes the same point in chapter 36 verses 23 to 25.

'For I will take you out of the nations, gather you from
all the lands and bring you back into your own land.
Then I will sprinkle clean water on you, and you will be
clean. I will cleanse you from all your filthiness and from
all your idols ...'

It is important to note that both these passages speak of
political restoration before spiritual restoration. Derek Prince
writes: 'The first part of restoration is political, but the end
purpose is spiritual-cleansing from all impurity ...'

We can therefore expect the Holy Spirit, in the years to
come, to intensify His work of banishing unbelief from Israel.
With this the prophet Zechariah agrees for he writes:

9

'And I will pour out on the house of David and on the inhabitants of Jerusalem the Spirit of grace and of supplication, so that they will look on Me whom they have pierced; and they will mourn for Him, as one mourns for an only son, and they will weep bitterly over Him, like the bitter weeping over a first-born ...'

(Zech. 12.10 NASB)

The historical prophets and restoration

Amos 3:7 declares that God: 'Does nothing unless He reveals His secret counsel to His servants the prophets ...'

Years before the physical restoration of Israel the prophets began to cry out, sometimes in what appeared to be a lonely wilderness, about Israel's regathering to the promised land. No doubt a deaf ear was turned in many circles because such a restoration seemed well nigh impossible. Derek Prince in his book, 'The Last Word on the Middle East', writes (speaking first of Israel's future spiritual restoration), 'Many people would dismiss this suggestion as inconceivable. And yet, a century earlier, just as many people would have dismissed as inconceivable the suggestion that the people of Israel would ever be restored to their land ...'

Nevertheless, the warnings were persistent and came from a multitude of prophets. God was true to His word, warning the world of Israel's soon-coming restoration before it happened. Somehow, by the power of the Holy Spirit, these 'prophets' sensed the way in which the wind of God's Spirit was blowing and they began to echo the words of Psalm 102:12–13:

'But Thou O Lord dost abide forever, and Thy name to all generations. Thou will arise and have compassion on Zion, for it is time to be gracious to her, for the appointed time has come ...'

The following is something of a short list of those who, in centuries gone by, began to preach and write about Israel's restoration to Palestine. In the seventeenth century a group of Christians, renowned for their zeal and piety and thus

The 'Shofar Horn', symbol of the trumpeting voice of God.

called 'Puritans', believed very strongly in Israel's future regathering to the promised land. Peter Toon, in his study of Puritan eschatology, states that the belief in the restoration of Israel was widely held among the Puritans of the seventeenth century.

In 1809, Faber published a book, the title of which partly read as follows: 'A general and connected view of the prophecies relative to the conversion, restoration, union and future glory of the houses of Judah and Israel ...'

In 1830, Lord Shaftesbury, an influential man and devout Christian, became a vigorous promoter of Jewish settlement in Palestine. Dwight Wilson, in his book, 'Armageddon Now', writes: '... he believed that Palestine actually belonged to the Jews and would be returned to them ...'

In 1853, Jacob J. Janeway, a professor of theology at the Presbyterian Western Seminary wrote: 'The Jews will be converted to the Christian faith, and settled and re-organised as a nation in the land of Palestine.'

John Cumming, a preacher of the Scottish National Church, published two prophetic books in 1855 which aroused great interest in the restoration of the Jews to Palestine. In one of these books he wrote: 'We may expect that the nations of the earth will begin ... to discuss in their cabinets the restoration of the Jews ...'

History has proved the accuracy of his statement!

In 1890, James H. Brookes, a Presbyterian pastor in St. Louis, 'pleaded for a literal interpretation of scripture and pointed out that the promised land of Israel was an unconditional promise ...'

Also, at this time a host of prophetic journals appeared all giving prominence to the restoration of Israel. Dwight Wilson's comment in this respect is worth noting: 'Prophetic magazines blossomed to help spread the scent of the "budding Fig Tree".' James H. Brookes published 'Truth' from 1875 to 1879. 'Prophetic Times' was edited by Joseph A. Seiss, president of the board of the Philadelphia Lutheran Theological Seminary and also editor of 'The Lutheran'. One of the points of the creed of 'Prophetic Times', which was published from 1863 to 1881, was, 'that in the new order of things to come, the house of Israel, or Jewish race, shall again occupy their own land and hold first place among the nations ...'

In 1878, H. Grattan Guinness, from England, published a book called, 'The Approaching End of the Age'. In this book he wrote of the soon coming restoration of Israel to Palestine.

Moreover, in 1886 an international prophetic conference held in Chicago released the following statement: 'History itself is Messianic. Events do not come to pass because predicted, but are predicted because ordained to come to pass ... The fortunes of Israel are, have been and will be precisely what God intends. A divine causality pervades all. Israel, already in the front in centuries gone by, shall be in the front again ...'

No doubt the most outstanding 'secular prophet' of this period was Theodor Herzl, regarded today as the father of modern day Zionism. In 1897, after the 'first world Zionist Congress' held in Basel, Switzerland, he said: 'At Basel I founded the Jewish State! If I said this out loud I would be greeted by universal laughter. In five years, perhaps, and certainly in 50 years, everyone will perceive it.'

These words were profoundly prophetic as exactly 50 years later the state of Israel was established. However, it is interesting to note that some of Herzl's staunchest supporters were English Christians known as 'restorationists'. Most notable among this group was a gentleman by the name of William Hechler.

He, convinced that the Bible predicted a restoration of the Jews to Palestine, gave his support to Herzl and encouraged him in every way possible in his Zionist endeavours. Of this remarkable man, Derek Prince writes: 'William Hechler, an Anglican clergyman and son of a Hebrew scholar, became convinced from his study of Bible prophecy that 1897 was a crucial year for the restoration of the Jewish state. Therefore, when he read Herzl's book, 'The Jewish State', he went directly to Herzl and put himself at Herzl's disposal to help bring the vision to reality ...'

Though Herzl was himself not religious it is nevertheless a fact that he frequently wrote of a supernatural compulsion in his work driving him to establish a Jewish homeland in Palestine.

In fact, this compulsion was so intense that on one occasion he wondered whether he had gone mad!

Lance Lambert, in his book, 'The Uniqueness of Israel', writes: 'For nine years, one single idea had possessed him – a determination that, somehow, somewhere, sometime, the Jewish people should again become a nation ...'

Finally, it is worth noting that the writings of C.I. Schofield at the end of the 19th century and beginning of the 20th were rather remarkable as to their accuracy concerning the restoration of Israel.

For instance, commenting on Romans 11:26, he wrote, 'According to the prophets, Israel regathered from all nations, restored to her own land and converted, is yet to have her greatest earthly exaltation and glory ... '

Yes, the prophets had caught the wind of the Spirit of God and the next century would witness the fulfilment of that which they had only greeted and perceived with spiritual eyes.

Indeed, the majority of them died in hope and trust knowing that they had faithfully discharged the responsibility that the prophetic mantle had laid upon them! God had declared His intentions to the world – the day of fulfilment was now at hand.

Historical events in restoration

The restoration of the Jewish state is characterised by some startling events that the sceptics of our world will, no doubt, pass off as coincidental. However, the honest enquirer will detect in all this the hand of God ... and hopefully the voice of God!

Indeed, so startling are these events that it almost seems that God is doing everything possible to catch our attention.

Here for your consideration are some of the most remarkable events:

1. William Hechler, a devout Christian, became convinced, through independent study of the Bible, that the year 1897 was crucial for Jewish restoration to Palestine.

    He was right, for in 1897 Theodor Herzl called the first world Jewish Congress since AD70, which met in Basel, Switzerland. At this congress Herzl proclaimed the restoration of the Jewish state. In fact, he opened the congress with these words, 'We are here to lay the foundation stone of the house which is to shelter the Jewish nation.'

2. In November 1917, Britain issued the Balfour declaration, paving the way for a Jewish homeland to be re-established in Palestine. The important part of this

declaration ran as follows: 'His Majesty's government views with favour the establishment in Palestine of a national home for the Jewish people . . .'

In that same month and year the Bolshevik revolution took place in Russia. It is surely no coincidence that this anti-God, wicked system destined to collide with Israel in the wilderness of Judea had its birth at the same time. The powers of darkness were playing what they deemed to be their trump card!

3. On 9th December 1917 General Allenby liberated Jerusalem from Turkish domination. On that same day the Jews lit their candles to celebrate the Feast of Hanukkah or the 'Festival of Lights', which commemorated the liberation of Jerusalem in 164BC by Judas Maccabees.

4. In 1948, on the 14th May, the State of Israel was proclaimed in Tel Aviv by David Ben Gurion.

This happened exactly 50 years after Herzl's prophetic statement in 1897. In scripture the 50th year is always the year of jubilee which requires that all property be turned over to the original owner! In 1948 a goodly portion of Palestine reverted back to Jewish control – the original owners.

5. In 1948, Hebrew – a dead language for almost 2000 years – was resurrected and proclaimed the official language of the Jewish State. This miraculous restoration of the Hebrew language was largely due to the tireless labours of Eliezer Ben Yehuda.

Lance Lambert writes: 'The task which confronted him was the rebirth of a language dead for many centuries. It was to cost him everything, but he lived to see his vision realised.'

Again, Lambert comments: 'No other language has hung on so slender a thread for its revival. It was virtually the life of one man and his family upon which the rebirth of Hebrew depended.'

Could the rebirth of the Hebrew language be the fulfilment of Zephaniah 3:9?

'... for then I will turn to the people a pure language, that they may all call upon the name of the Lord, to serve Him with one consent ...'

6. In 1967, during the now famous Six Day War of June, Jerusalem was liberated and placed under Israel's sovereignty. This incredible event not only gave Jewish jurisdiction over Jerusalem for the first time in 2100 years, but it also marked the fulfilment of Jesus's prophetic statement recorded in Luke 21:24:

    '... and they – the Jews – will fall by the edge of the sword and will be led captive into all nations and Jerusalem will be trampled underfoot by the Gentiles until the times of the Gentiles be fulfilled ...'

    This happened exactly 50 years after Allenby first liberated Jerusalem from the Turks in 1917. Again, 1967 just happened to be the year of Jubilee, which requires all property to be returned to the original owners!

7. Since the proclamation of the State of Israel in 1948 this tiny nation, no bigger than the American State of New Jersey, has been called upon to defend itself in no less than five wars in order to survive. That is – in 1948, 1956, 1967, 1973 and 1982. This miraculous preservation can only be attributed to one thing – the hand of God! Indeed in the future she will no doubt have to fight many more battles, but our confidence in a covenant-keeping God is such that we know in the end she will emerge victorious, redeemed and secure.

As we then consider these remarkable historical events, the conclusion we come to is clear: Israel is not a modern day political accident. No, she exists because of God's faithfulness and commitment to His word.

Lance Lambert writes: 'Israel is no political accident but evidence to the nations that God is true, that His word is accurate, reliable and relevant. The Lord intends to vindicate Himself, His authority and His word in a manner which leaves the nations of the world without excuse ...'

16

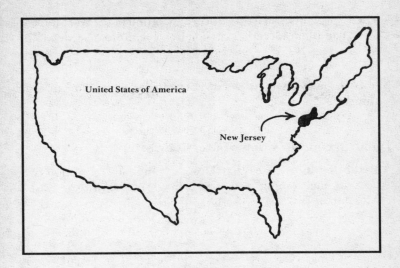

The State of New Jersey, almost the exact size of Israel. Both enjoy a land mass of approximately 13,000 km².

The implications of restoration

Romans chapter 11 indicates that we should long and pray for Israel's complete restoration. That is – restoration to the land and restoration to the Lord, as this will mean great blessing for Israel: She will be exalted as the foremost of the nations and it will mean great blessing for the church and for the earth.

v11 'I say then, they did not stumble so as to fall, did they? May it never be! But by their transgression salvation has come to the Gentiles, to make them jealous.

v12 Now, if their transgression be riches for the world and their failure be riches for the Gentiles, how much more will their fulfilment be!

v13 But I am speaking to you who are Gentiles. Inasmuch then as I am an apostle of the Gentiles, I magnify my ministry.

v14 If somehow I might move to jealousy my fellow countrymen and save some of them.

v15 For if their rejection be reconciliation of the world, what will their acceptance be, but life from the dead?' – verses 11–15

It is clear, then, that Israel's restoration will mean four things:

The Second Coming of Messiah Jesus

Psalm 102:16 declares that Israel's complete restoration will lead to the coming a second time of Jesus the promised Messiah of Israel.

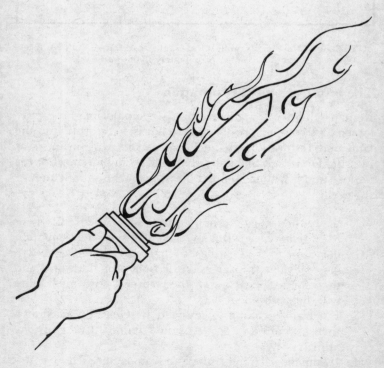

The implications of restoration!

'For the Lord has built up Zion, He has appeared in His glory . . .'

Moreover, in Matthew 23:39 Jesus Himself declared that Israel would not see Him again until she would find it in her heart to welcome Him as Messiah.

'. . . For I say to you, from now on you shall not see Me until you say, "Blessed is He who comes in the name of the Lord . . ."'

The first step toward this glorious day of Jesus's return has been accomplished for she, that is Israel, is back in her land. All that remains now is for the veil of unbelief to be lifted from her spiritual eyes. That day can't be too far off!

Even Paul confessed that her unbelief or hardening would only be partial – that is, not for ever. Yes, a new day is just

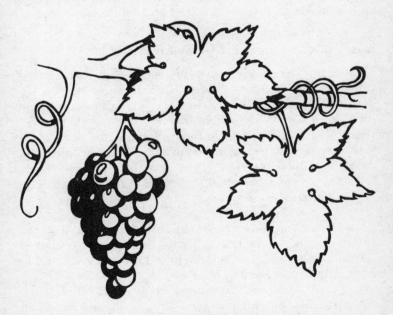

Israel fully restored ... a day of new power for the church.

around the corner. Israel's present restoration declares and confirms it.

A new demonstration of Divine power

In our passage of scripture, quoted from Romans 11, it will be noted that Paul writes that Israel's restoration will mean something more wonderful than the present divine riches that the church has experienced (v12). Further down in the passage he says that this 'something more wonderful' will be like 'life from the dead' (v15).

Basically this can only mean that a new breath of resurrection life will come into the community of God when Israel's restoration is complete.

Another way of putting it is to say that the Church without restored Israel is like a rugby team without its star player. When the star player returns to the team a new zeal and power floods the players. Thus will it be when Israel shakes off her 'partial hardening' and returns to the team.

A day of exaltation and glory for Israel

Age-old promises made to Israel by a covenant-keeping God will be fulfilled in that day. With her King enthroned on Mt. Zion her borders will be extended, her righteousness will shine forth like a bright light, her revelation – that is, the Word of the Lord – will encompass the globe causing all nations to bask in the light thereof and she will be exalted in the sight of the nations.

And if we don't believe this then what is the meaning of Zechariah 14:16?

> 'Then it will come about that any who are left of all the nations that went against Jerusalem will go up from year to year to worship the King, the Lord of Hosts, and to celebrate the Feast of Booths.
>
> And it will be that whichever of the families of the earth does not go up to Jerusalem to worship the King, the Lord of Hosts, there will be no rain on them ...'

20

A day of glory.

And, what is the meaning of Zechariah 8:22–23?

'So many peoples and mighty nations will come to seek the Lord of Hosts in Jerusalem and to entreat the favour of the Lord. Thus says the Lord of Hosts, In those days ten men from the nations of every language will grasp the garment of a Jew saying, "Let us go with you, for we have heard that God is with you …"'

And, finally, let us note Zechariah 8:3

'Thus says the Lord, I will return to Zion and will dwell in the midst of Jerusalem. Then Jerusalem will be called the City of Truth, and the mountain of the Lord of Hosts will be called the Holy Mountain …'

A day of universal peace

There will be no peace in our world until the Prince of Peace, Jesus Christ, reigns as King over the nations. That glorious day is dependent upon Israel's restoration for He will not come to reign until she invites Him back.
(Matthew 23:39)

'Shalom' for the world.

The true peacemakers of the world are those, then, that work for the preservation and full restoration of Israel. In short, to bring the King back means to first bring His people back from dispersion and unbelief.

For this reason Jerusalem is called, 'The City of Peace' and God's people are to pray for her peace and restoration.

> 'Pray for the peace of Jerusalem:
> May they prosper who love you
> May peace be within your walls
> And prosperity within your palaces'
>
> (Psalm 122.6–7 NASB)

The true 'United Nations' is thus Jerusalem. It is therefore not surprising that the forces of darkness are constantly intent on her destruction and spiritual poverty for in this way they can rob the world of 'Shalom' – peace!

In recognition of this truth, Milton Lindbert writes concerning the Church's responsibility in the world: '... they will not be unmindful of God's chosen people whose future is intimately bound up with the welfare of all the world. In fact a clear comprehension of God's programme and a single-hearted devotion to it must cause believers to place this key nation foremost in loving consideration and earnest endeavour.'

The present ongoing restoration of Israel heralds the soon-coming era of a new world order based on righteousness. This is the world's only hope. Indeed the restoration and preservation of Israel as a nation is the world's only visible and real guarantee that this new day is about to dawn. How strange it is, therefore, that the majority of nations of this world are bent on her destruction. The words of Jesus apply to them, 'They do not know the things that make for peace.' Luke 19:42.

The prophet was therefore right when he said:

> '... It is Zion, no one cares for her ...'
>
> (Jeremiah 30:17b NASB)

However, just before that tragic commentary on the world's attitude to Israel, he affirms that God cares for her and is committed to her restoration.

> '... For I will restore you to health, and I will heal you of your wounds,' declares the Lord, 'because they have called you an outcast ...'   (Jeremiah 30:17a NASB)

God is a 'Zionist' – it therefore behoves every Christian to be one too!

Chapter 2

The covenants of Israel

The emergence of Israel among the family of nations is a startling development – especially in view of the fact that history denies such a possibility in that no other nation of antiquity has been exiled twice only to survive and be restored again. It is also startling because she has emerged into a world that basically doesn't want her. In the halls of government she is condemned and rejected as an intruder or 'foreign body'.

Yet despite all this she nevertheless commands a central place in the world's media. Derek Prince says: 'since the end of World War Two the focus of world politics has shifted from Europe and North America to the Middle East. Today's news media devote more attention to the Middle East than to any other area on earth.'

Israel, as we have already pointed out, is no bigger than the American State of New Jersey ... so what draws the attention of the world to her borders? Or as another enquirer put it: 'Why has this tiny struggling land become the fulcrum of all human history?'

The answer to this question is twofold:

1. Because of the strategic position of Israel in the East West conflict in which oil is a major issue, and
2. Because of the action of a faithful living God – the God of Israel.

The first answer is really an outflow or result of the second answer, namely: Israel exists because of the faithfulness of a covenant-keeping God. Though the world is loathe to accept this reality it is still nevertheless true.

Her restoration is therefore because of theological realities and we need to be fully acquainted with them. In short, Israel exists because God exists and thus God is prepared to honour His word and His promises. Such promises were made to Israel in the form of covenants. Two such covenants require investigation for us to adequately understand what the present day world calls 'The Middle East Conflict'.

The Abrahamic Covenant

This covenant mentioned on more than one occasion in the book of Genesis was initiated by God. It was one-sided – that is, God declared the terms and benefits. It was also unconditional and everlasting.

> 'On that day the Lord made a covenant with Abram saying, "To your descendants I have given this land, from the river of Egypt as far as the great river, the river Euphrates ..."' (Genesis 15:18 NASB)

Again in Genesis 13:14–15 we read:

> 'And the Lord said to Abram, after Lot had separated from him, "Now lift up your eyes and look from the place where you are, northward and southward and eastward and westward, for all the land which you see, I will give it to you and to your descendants forever ..."'

An examination of this covenant reveals the following:

The covenant is initiated by God and as such is unconditional. Most expositors are in agreement with this point (Note Walvoord's comment at the end of the chapter) but, if any conditions do exist they are as follows. That Abram should leave Ur of the Chaldeans and walk uprightly before

The Abrahamic Covenant.

God (See Genesis 12:1–3 and Genesis 17:1–7). If such conditions did exist there is no doubt that they have been fully met, leaving God to keep His side of the covenant.

The covenant bequeaths certain well-defined territories to Israel as an everlasting possession – that is, the land between the Red Sea and the Euphrates River is hers forever. God has given it to them ... and nothing can change that! Indeed in Exodus 23:31 the clear boundaries of this tract of land are spelled out again just in case we doubt it.

> 'And I will fix your boundary from the Red Sea to the Sea of the Philistines, and from the wilderness to the river Euphrates, for I will deliver the inhabitants of the land into your hand, and you will drive them out before you ...'

The implications of all this are clear. Namely, irrespective of the fortunes of history, God is bound or obligated to ensure, as a result of this covenant, that when present history closes Israel is secure in this selfsame tract of land.

This is even more true when we consider that the full

extent of this land has never as yet been settled by Israel. Not even Solomon's glorious reign saw Israel settled as far north as the Euphrates River. Considering these implications, the Assemblies of God publication, 'The Evangel', once stated: 'We need not guess or be ignorant concerning Israel's future, for it is the one nation whose history has been written in advance ...'

Yes, Israel must return to her land and occupy it. The present restoration of the State of Israel is the first step toward the final and full implementation of the Abrahamic Covenant.

The issues are clear. The Abrahamic Covenant, one of the outstanding covenants in the Word of God, promises Israel a permanent existence as a nation. This being so, the church is not fulfilling Israel's promises, but rather Israel as a nation has a future yet in prospect, and the Abrahamic Covenant promises Israel permanent possession of the promised land. This means that Israel must yet come into possession of the land, for she has never fully possessed it in her history.

The Abrahamic Covenant therefore guarantees the preservation of the nation of Israel and it is for this reason that God declares the following in Jeremiah 31:35–37:

> 'Thus says the Lord, "Who gives the sun for light by day, and the fixed order of the moon and the stars for light by night. Who stirs up the sea so that its waves roar; the Lord of Hosts is His name. If this fixed order departs from Me," declares the Lord, "then the offspring of Israel also shall cease from being a nation before Me for ever."
>
> 'Thus says the Lord, "If the heavens above can be measured, and the foundations of the earth searched out below, then I will also cast off all the offspring of Israel for all that they have done," declares the Lord.'

All this simply means that God will never cast them off and they will always be a nation before Him.

Speaking of the Abrahamic Covenant, Dwight Pentecost in his book, 'Things to Come', writes: 'This covenant then determines the whole future programme for the nation Israel and is a major factor in biblical eschatology . . .'

'The King's Business', an important prophetic journal, once stated: 'But the end is determined. Palestine is for the Jew. The land is Israel's – not by reason of Great Britain's pledge, but by divine decree. The Abrahamic Covenant, not the Balfour Declaration, is the Jewish Magna Charta to the land of Palestine . . .'

In the final analysis therefore, if any aspect of the Abrahamic Covenant fails, then the credibility, integrity and revelation of God as God becomes suspect.

Derek Prince in his book, 'The Last Word on the Middle East', writes of Israel's restoration: 'This is no accident. God has raised a banner for the nations. He has gained their attention, and is now speaking to them through it. What is He saying? I believe God intends to focus the attention of the world on two things: His Word and His covenant. Concerning His Word, God is saying to the nations, "The Bible, My Word is a true, relevant, up-to-date book. Its predictions are still being fulfilled today with absolute accuracy."

'Concerning His covenant, God is saying, "I am a God Who keeps My covenant. Four thousand years ago I made a covenant with Abraham and with his descendants after him. I promised never to break that covenant, and I have never broken it. That covenant is still in force today, and I am now causing it to be worked out through the course of human history . . .""

In other words, the importance of Israel to us as Christian people is this: If God is unfaithful to them He can be unfaithful to us. Or, if God can break His covenant with them what guarantee do we have that He will not break His covenant with us?

The answer to this question is clear. Our guarantee is His faithful dealings with Israel in history. He has faithfully kept covenant with them and as we take note of this we are assured that He will keep covenant with us who 'have fled for refuge in laying hold of the hope set before us.'

The comments of Elmer A. Josephson are worth noting in this respect for in his book, 'Israel God's Key to World

Redemption', he writes: '. . . it is an absolute essential to take an inventory of Israel's past, since it does and will involve the future and destiny of the whole world. Israel is the Almighty's model, a slide-rule nation and laboratory in which the Almighty's law and word have been tested.'

All in all then, the Abrahamic Covenant with Israel is thus of vital importance to the Christian and, believe it or not, it is at the root of the present political events in the Middle East.

Moreover, in bringing this section to an end may I bring to your attention the fact that the writer of the New Testament book of Hebrews affirms that we, as Christian people, can count God faithful because He has kept His covenant with Abraham.

> 'For when God made the promise to Abraham, since He could swear by no one greater, He swore by Himself, saying, "I will surely bless you, and I will surely multiply you."
>
> And thus, having patiently waited, he obtained the promise. For men swear by one greater than themselves, and with them an oath given as confirmation is an end of every dispute. In the same way God, desiring even more to show to the heirs of the promise the unchangeableness of His purpose, interposed with an oath, in order that by two unchangeable things, in which it is impossible for God to lie, we may have strong encouragement, we who have fled for refuge in laying hold of the hope set before us.
>
> This hope we have as an anchor of the soul, a hope both sure and steadfast and one which enters within the veil, where Jesus has entered as a forerunner for us . . .'
>
> (Hebrews 6:13–20 NASB)

The Palestinian Covenant

> 'So it shall become when all of these things have come upon you, the blessing and the curse which I have set before you, and you call them to mind in all nations where the Lord your God has banished you, and you

30

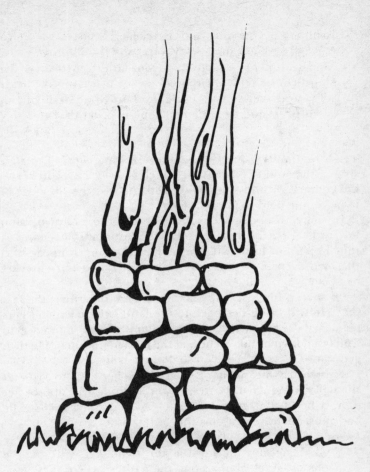

The Palestinian Covenant.

return to the Lord your God and obey Him with all your
heart and soul according to all that I command you
today, you and your sons, then the Lord your God will
restore you from captivity, and have compassion on you,
and will gather you again from all peoples where the
Lord your God has scattered you.

If your outcasts are at the ends of the earth, from
there He will bring you back. And the Lord your God

will bring you into the land which your fathers possessed, and you shall possess it; and He will prosper you and multiply you more than your fathers. Moreover the Lord your God will circumcise your heart and the heart of your descendants, to love the Lord your God with all your heart and with all your soul, in order that you may live.' (Deut. 30:1–6 NASB)

The Abrahamic Covenant gave everlasting right of ownership of the land of Canaan to Israel. However, obedience to the commands and statutes of God ensured the privilege of living in the land that was theirs.

In short, disobedience would not mean loss of ownership but rather loss of domicile. The 'Palestinian Covenant' is thus important in that it affirms Israel's everlasting right to the land even if, because of disobedience and unrighteousness, she is not living in it!

Of special interest is the fact that God underlines the fact that He will bring her back to the land 'which your fathers possessed'. This is a clear and unmistakable reference to Canaan. Having thus identified the land in question, He then goes on to say: '... and you shall possess it.'

This clearly means that if God brings her back to the land she will reconquer it, possess it and nothing will uproot her from it because it is hers. Ezekiel, speaking of Israel's exile and subsequent return, has this to say:

'... Thus says the Lord God, "Behold, I will take the sons of Israel from among the nations where they have gone, and I will gather them from every side and bring them into their own land ...

"And they shall live on the land that I gave to Jacob My servant, in which your fathers lived; and they will live on it, they, and their sons, and their sons, forever, and David My servant shall be their prince forever ..."'
(Ezekiel 37:21–25 NASB)

Again it is to be noted that the intentions of God are clear. Israel's exile in no way means loss of possession of the land.

No, the land has been given to Jacob and his descendants and this is so 'forever'.

History agrees with this, as Israel has been judged and exiled twice. However, she has also returned twice to the same tract of land. In 586 BC she was exiled to Babylon only to return nearly seventy years later under the leadership of Ezra and Nehemiah.

In AD 70 she was judged again and dispersed throughout the world – in fact, to its four corners. But she returned again, in 1948, to take her place among the nations of the world. Indeed, the prophet Isaiah clearly spoke of just such a twofold dispersion and regathering and at the same time implied that her second exile would be the last.

> 'Then it will happen on that day that the Lord will again recover the second time with His hand the remnant of His people, who will remain from Assyria, Egypt, Pathros, Cush, Elam, Shinar, Hamath and from the islands of the sea.
> 'And He will lift up a standard for the nations and will assemble the banished ones of Israel, and will gather the dispersed of Judah from the four corners of the earth . . .'

In a certain sense therefore, as far as God is concerned, the Middle East conflict has been solved. Israel will possess the land and that's the end of the matter. This is the abiding message of the 'Palestinian Covenant'. The Palestine Liberation Organisation and even Russia are destined for failure and destruction because there is a God in heaven who cannot lie and who keeps His Word or covenant.

Dwight Pentecost, in his book, 'Things to Come' writes of Canaan: '. . . God not only guarantees its possession to them but obligates Himself to judge and remove all Israel's enemies . . .'

This unbelievable commitment of God to Israel is thus the one way in which the world can distinguish the true God from the false in that the overwhelming odds against Israel make her survival impossible without Divine help.

The prophet Ezekiel, speaking of Israel's soon-coming battle with 'Gog of the land of Magog', and her subsequent preservation and victory, because of Divine help, describes the result as follows:

> 'And I shall magnify Myself, sanctify Myself, and make Myself known in the sight of many nations, and they will know that I am the Lord ...'   (Ezekiel 38:23 NASB)

We the gentiles, who have trusted in this God, are wonderfully assured and encouraged as we see Him, the God of Israel, pushing aside nations and empires in order to keep His word and promises to Israel. The 'New York Prophetic Conference' released this statement after the First World War: '... It seems then clear that Divine providence has used this horrible war to take Palestine from the Turk and make it possible for the Jewish people to return ...'

The same statement could have been released after the Second World War as, out of the shambles and horror of that war, emerged the state of Israel on the 14th May 1948.

Nations were uprooted, overthrown, judged and pushed aside because of their sin and unrighteousness and yet, somehow, in it all God was also honouring His covenants with Israel. So the words of one author sum up the situation adequately: 'Just as it had taken World War I to prepare the promised land for the Jewish people, it took World War 2 to prepare the people for the promised land ...'

Covenants and morality

For many, the emergence of the state of Israel has aroused serious moral questions. For them the return of the Jews to Palestine is seen as having inflicted hardship and suffering upon the Arab peoples who were living there. These peoples, in their opinion, have been robbed of their land, leaving them displaced and eventually ending up as refugees. The question is therefore asked: 'Would God keep His covenant with Israel in such a way that many Arab peoples are called upon to endure untold hardship and suffering?' In their opinion the

34

**The Abrahamic and Palestinian Covenants –
still moulding the Middle East today.**

answer is 'No', as, if He did, it would be inconsistent with
His character which, in His Word, is revealed as being just,
righteous and loving.

This also means that they deny any divine action in the
restoration of the Jewish state, concluding at the same time
that the whole affair is a political accident – albeit a miraculous one at that!

The executive secretary of the Southern Baptist Conference in America once said: 'This new nation, Israel, is a miracle. In honesty, I must add that it is an immoral miracle.' And Morris Zeidman, writing in the Assemblies of God publication, 'The Evangel', said: 'My sympathies are with the Jews and I believe that Palestine has been promised by both God and men to the Jewish people, but the methods that are being used today to make Palestine a Jewish state cannot be considered Christian and therefore I believe are not of God.'

Those, then, like the author of this book, who believe that Israel's restoration is of God, have to answer this apparent moral dilemma. In my opinion there is a just biblical answer. Scripture is clear in many passages that Israel's return to Palestine is to be in unbelief (See Chapter One sub-heading, 'The scriptures and restoration'). This being so, can we expect her to return in such a way that she applies 'born-again' or Christian ethics to her politics? The answer is, clearly, 'No'. In the light of this, is Zeidman's lament that their actions are not 'Christian' justified? Again, I think not!

However, this in no way means that we condone the apparent evil, suffering and hardship that has come to the Arab peoples because of Israel's restoration. No, it is my belief that God always acts justly and righteously. Therefore a view of Israel's return has to be held that is in harmony with God's character and scripture. Such a view is certainly propounded in the pages of the Bible.

For instance, Nebuchadnezzar's devastating invasion of Israel, culminating in the ruthless killing of men, women and children and Israel's exile in 586 BC was said to be an act of God!

'The oracle concerning Babylon which Isaiah the son of Amoz saw. Lift up a standard on the bare hill, raise your voice to them, wave the hand that they may enter the doors of the nobles. I have commanded My consecrated ones, I have even called My mighty warriors, My proudly exulting one, To execute My anger ...'

Here God calls the Chaldean army, 'My consecrated ones'

and 'My mighty warriors'. Having thus described them He
then goes on to describe their divine mission:

> 'Anyone who is found will be thrust through, and any-
> one who is captured will fall by the sword. Their little
> ones also will be dashed to pieces before their eyes, their
> houses will be plundered and their wives ravished . . .'
> (Isaiah 13:1–3: 15–16 NASB)

So God's instruments are not always those that apply
'Christian principles' to their actions. The prophet Habakkuk found himself in the same moral dilemma as our 20th
century moralists have found themselves, in connection with
the modern state of Israel. Only today the 'invaders' are not
Chaldeans but Jews. Nevertheless, Habakkuk considered
God's use of the ruthless Babylonians to be inconsistent with
His character and felt it necessary to remind God that His
holiness is such that it cannot gaze upon wickedness or
unrighteousness. His utter dismay that God should do such a
thing is expressed in these words:

> 'Thou, O Lord has appointed them (The Babylonians)
> to judge; and Thou, O Rock, has established them to
> correct. Thine eyes are too pure to approve evil, and
> Thou canst not look on wickedness with favour. Why
> dost Thou look with favour on those who deal
> treacherously?' (Habakkuk 1:12–13 NASB)

In short, the prophet was saying, 'How can a righteous
God use unrighteous people as His instruments?' The facts
are that He did, as the Babylonians were evil pagans, certainly void of 'Christian principles' or righteous ethics.
Moreover, the Babylonian army was far more ruthless than
that of the modern state of Israel. In fact, Nebuchadnezzar's
brutality makes any brutality perpetrated by Israel look
angelic!

Why then did a righteous God see fit to use the
unrighteous Babylonians? The answer is clear: because of
Israel's sin, unrighteousness and rebellion. Indeed, the

prophet Habakkuk soon came to recognise this. Israel had apostacised, now judgment was inevitable.

Also, Joshua's invasion of Canaan round about 1300 BC was also ruthless. Men, women and children were put to the sword and whole cities were blotted out. Who was behind it? Scripture leaves us in no doubt. God was! He was giving His people possession of the promised land. Surely this was immoral?

The answer again is 'No', as the wickedness of the inhabitants of the land had become such that it was ripe for judgment. In fact, scripture affirms that God delayed 'invasion day' until such time as the sin of the Canaanites, Hittites, Jebusites, etc, demanded Divine retribution.

'Then in the fourth generation they shall return here, for the iniquity of the Amorite is not yet complete.'
(Genesis 15:16, also Leviticus 18:24–28 NASB)

In this way God ensured that in keeping His covenant with Abraham He was also, at the same time, dealing righteously with the inhabitants of the land. Why should this not be true today? I believe that it is, for God always acts in the 'fulness of time' and His covenant and character have not changed.

Israel's present 'invasion' of the land is to be seen in this light and therefore the modern protestations raised concerning Israel's return and the resultant displacement of so-called 'Palestinians' is nothing more than an inadequate grasp of the principles of righteousness which God applies to nations.

Those who question Israel's second return to the land must at the same time be prepared to question the morality of her first conquest under Joshua. After all, there's no difference except that which is created by time.

If God was honouring the Abrahamic Covenant then, which resulted in killing and destruction, why is it considered untenable if He honours it today? This God surely must do as it is an everlasting covenant.

Moreover, let us be careful not to accuse God of perpetrating evil in order to honour His covenant. In the miraculous economy of God, historical circumstances become such that they are right for judgment and restoration. God in His infinite wisdom is able to bring these two acts together in such a way that His eternal purposes are worked out. (Genesis 15:13–14. Notice how judgment and restoration are harmonised.)

At the same time His dealings with all men are just and righteous. In all this Israel is not given a licence to kill and destroy as she pleases, and I do not think for one moment that Israel has such intentions. Indeed her human rights record is one of the best in the world. Also, it does not mean that we as Christians should sit idly by and condone human suffering. It is to be noted that God always judges those who seek to further the process of judgment. Sometimes our silence does this. (Zechariah 1:14–15.)

We are therefore not to be so supportive of Israel's restoration that we ignore injustice and sin. In all this there is a very delicate balance and God expects us as Christian people to act and think as those who know and love His word. However, we do affirm, as Daniel the prophet declares, that God exalts kingdoms and nations and then brings them down as He sees fit (Daniel 2:20–21). The fall of such kingdoms is said to be because of their sin and unrighteousness (Proverbs 14:34). Indeed, in regard to the Middle East, no one can deny that Islamic rule has always been a very cruel and wicked thing. If you don't believe me then try living in Tehran for a while and you will soon discover the real nature of the Ayatollah's benevolence! Be assured, his type of Islamic rule is not abnormal or extreme. Rather, it is the revival of orthodox Muhammedism. A casual glance at history will confirm this. Moreover, if the present revival of Islam is allowed to spread unchecked, the Middle East will be thrown into a new age of intolerance and barbarism. It is no secret that Islam seeks to destroy Christianity and Judaism.

In the final analysis then, it must be recognised that displaced persons, wherever they occur in the world, must be helped to establish a normal lifestyle again. Our Christian commitment demands this and we would be failing if we neglected our responsibility in this respect.

Yet it must also be affirmed that Israel has a divine right to the land of Canaan that she now occupies. Much of this land she gained because she was called upon to defend herself in five wars in which she was not the aggressor.

The War of Independence in 1948 was initiated by the Arabs in defiance of the United Nations resolution which determined Israel's borders and recognised her existence as a state. The same was true in 1956, 1967 and 1973, the last-mentioned being a glaring instance of Arab aggression as the now famous 'Yom Kippur War' erupted at a time when Israel only had a skeleton force defending her borders.

The facts prior to the 1948 and 1967 wars are also worth noting as it is well known that Arab propaganda, broadcast over the radio, encouraged all Arabs living in Israel to forsake their homes and flee. This was done because it was promised that in a few days the collective Arab might would crush Israel, liberate Palestine and not only return their homes but also give them the liberated Jewish ones.

Thousands of Arabs living in Israel left their homes before the ensuing conflict only to end up as refugees in Jordan, Gaza and elsewhere. Those that stayed were offered Israeli citizenship. They now enjoy equality before the law and have flourished alongside their Jewish partners. It is no secret that Arabs living in Israel are far better off than their 'brothers' in neighbouring Arab countries!

Moreover, their 'oil rich brothers' have done nothing to assist the Arab refugees, simply because if they did they would lose their lever against Israel. The truth is, the Palestinian refugees are convenient fodder to be fed constantly to the cattle of the Arab cause (which amounts to Jewish genocide). The Arabs themselves care very little, if anything, about their plight.

One last point about the land in question is worth noting here. It is not true to suggest that Israel 'grabbed' or confiscated land in Palestine from the Arabs in order to expand her territorial sovereignty. The truth is that a good portion of the land was bought for outrageous prices from the Arab owners themselves.

In bringing this chapter to a close, I would like to affirm the following:

In the restoration of the State of Israel, we recognise Divine faithfulness to a covenant made 4000 years ago with Abraham. This covenant is eternal and irrevocable. However, in the act of restoration we also discern the right-eous judgment of God upon those nations that have acted wickedly during their occupation of the land belonging to Israel.

As Christian people, we shall not seek to further God's judgment in any way, either by actively seeking to eject Arabs from Israel or by being supportive of such endeavours if they occur or by maintaining a position of support for Israel that totally ignores sin and unrighteousness in that land.

We shall also not be silent concerning the suffering of Arab peoples. Rather we should seek to help suffering peoples wherever they are to be found in our world, always assuring them of God's love and willingness to receive them through repentance and faith in Messiah Jesus.

Moreover, the restoration of the Jewish state does not mean that God loves Jews and hates Arabs. This possible thought or attitude has to be guarded against. Rather, it simply means that God honours His contracts – as we are expected to do in life – whilst at the same time He loves all men everywhere.

Perhaps the only fitting way to end this chapter would be to quote the words of an Arab Christian:

'I want my people, the Arabs, to be blessed. That is why I stand by God's people, the Jews, who I believe should return to the land of Israel. Some may think that by loving and supporting Israel, they cannot also love the Arab people. That is not true. God's covenant with Israel was the starting point for a plan of salvation that reaches to all mankind. Arab believers in Jesus Christ need not feel threatened or inferior to Jews because, in Him, we have equal access to God's blessings ...'

(Mrs Van der Hoeven
Arab Christian born in Sudan)

41

Walvoord says:

> *The Abrahamic Covenant is confirmed repeatedly by reiteration and enlargement. In none of these instances are any of the added promises conditioned upon the faithfulness of Abraham's seed or of Abraham himself . . . nothing is said about it being conditioned upon the future faithfulness of either Abraham or his seed . . . '*

Chapter 3

The sufferings of Israel

'For they are Thy people and Thine inheritance which Thou hast brought forth from Egypt, from the midst of the iron furnace ...'
(I Kings 8:51 NASB)

The sufferings of the Jewish people are unexplainable and a mystery if we do not understand the spiritual issues involved. Sadly, many do not appreciate these issues and still others are not willing to face them ... and even seek to deny them.

For instance, many Christians, even to this present day, see no future for Israel in the plan of God. The restoration of the state is a political accident and the church has now inherited all the blessings promised to Israel. The curses however still apply conveniently to Israel!

By the way, one speaker at a conference held in Jerusalem recently asked: 'If Israel is a political accident, as many Christians believe, is Jesus returning to the capital of a political accident?'

There is no denying therefore that the 'finished theology' has made anti-Semitism more easy and more acceptable in the church. This, in turn, has contributed greatly to the appalling suffering that God's ancient people have had to endure through history. The awful periods of the Crusaders, the Spanish Inquisition and the pogroms of Russia are but a few examples of anti-Semitism perpetrated by the church.

And, lest we pass these instances off as being irrelevant in that they do not represent the 'born-again church', let us never forget that history affirms that many godly, born-again men of God were guilty of anti-Semitism and publicly denounced the Jews as 'Christ-killers'.

Moreover, the appalling and horrific slaughter of six million Jews by Hitler during the Second World War was made possible in many ways by the anti-Semetic preaching of Martin Luther some centuries before. For instance, in 1543 Luther wrote a book called 'Of Jews and Their Lies'. In this book he stated the following: 'What should we Christians do now with this contemptible, damned people the Jews? I will give my true advice. First, that their synagogues and schools be set on fire. Second, that their houses similarly be razed and destroyed, for they practise the same ill things in them as in their schools. Third, that their prayer books and Talmudics be taken from them. Fourth, that their rabbis be forbidden on peril of their lives henceforth to teach, that safe conduct and the right to earn a living be entirely taken from them and precious things such as they have, be stolen from them . . .' The Nazis found Luther's sermons very inspiring and actually quoted portions of them in order to justify their evil deeds. The Russians are doing the very same thing today in their persecution of Soviet Jewry. S. M. Meacham in her book, 'It Is Still Not Too Late', concerning the plight of Soviet Jewry, writes: 'There is an established link between Nazi propaganda and the current Soviet campaign of hate . . .'

Modern theologians continue to sow the same seeds of evil and destruction as they propagate a 'no future for Israel, theology'. For instance, two New Testament commentators have written:

> 'An internal necessity impelled the Jewish people to nail Jesus to the cross because He destroyed their pretentions. Israel is maintained as a people, as a race, for the day of judgment to come.'

It will be noted that as far as these two theologians are

Israel, the suffering servant of God in the world.

concerned, Israel's preservation, conceded to be miraculous, is however not for salvation as Paul writes in Romans 11, but for slaughter! They are finished, cursed and forgotten forever. Indeed as far back as 1929 Moody Monthly 'admitted that the historical position of the church for centuries had been that the Jews had lost their chance and that there was to be no restoration of a national Israel but only a spiritual Israel – the church . . .'

This sinful attitude of the church and the response that it brought is one inadequate yet real answer to their historical sufferings. The fuller answer is to be found in the spiritual world of wickedness, as the enormity of their sufferings must force us to look in this direction.

In the final analysis their sufferings have no earthly or human explanation. Something 'other worldly' is attempting to destroy the Jewish nation and this 'something' has sought to influence men and women in this regard. For instance, only a demon-possessed person would state, as Nazi Julius Streicher did, '. . . that the Jews are children of the devil and murderers of mankind. Whoever is a murderer deserves to be killed himself . . .'

Moreover, if this 'something' is so desperate to destroy them, then surely it is because they hold the key to some vital plan of God for the world. In short this 'something' is demonic and it knows that their destruction would mean the end of God's plan for world redemption.

In this respect Revelation 12:1–6 agrees. Speaking of Israel, John writes:

> 'And a great sign appeared in heaven. A woman clothed with the sun, and the moon under her feet, and on her head a crown of twelve stars, and she was with child, and she cried out, being in labor and in pain to give birth. And another sign appeared in heaven and behold a great red dragon having seven heads and ten horns and on his heads were seven diadems. And his tail swept away a third of the stars of heaven, and threw them to the earth. And the dragon stood before the woman who was about to give birth, so that when she gave birth he might devour her child. And she gave birth to a son, a male child, who is to rule all the nations with a rod of iron, and her child was caught up to God and to His throne.'

The 'woman' here mentioned is clearly Israel as the reference to the woman clothed with the sun, etc, refers back to Genesis 37:9, which in turn obviously refers to Jacob and his twelve sons. Also, only the nation Israel has given birth to a Son, Jesus, who will rule the world with a rod of iron. The dragon obviously refers to the devil who has sought to destroy Israel through the seven anti-God gentile empires of history, these being Egypt, Assyria, Babylon, Media-Persia, Greece, Rome and the soon-coming revived Roman empire.

The Bible is, therefore, more than clear about the real

source of Israel's sufferings. It is a demonic one and this means that her sufferings are!

Bound up with her calling

Way back in eternity God realised that man would exercise his free will to rebel against God, so side with the devil and thus become the slave of sin. However, God nevertheless determined to rescue man from the tragedy of his free will choice.

To do this it was necessary to choose out a nation from all the world through which God could bring the revelation of His word and, more important still, through which God could eventually channel a Saviour who would redeem the world from loss.

A nation was vital to God's plan of saving the world for without it a godly revelation and heritage would never be preserved! National heritage is a very powerful thing. A nation whose heritage is the pure revelation of God would certainly be proud of it and do everything possible to preserve it.

Thus the revelation and understanding of God embodied in a nation would be protected, preserved and given as a light to all generations and nations of the world. This nation was Israel.

Referring to Israel, Isaiah writes:

> 'Arise, shine, for your light has come, and the glory of the Lord has risen upon you. For behold, darkness will cover the earth and deep darkness the peoples, but the Lord will rise upon you, and His glory will appear upon you. And nations will come to your light, and kings to the brightness of your rising ...' (Isaiah 60:1–3 NASB)

And again Isaiah writes:

> 'And now says the Lord, who formed me from the womb to be His servant, to bring Jacob back to Him, in order that Israel might be gathered to Him, for I am honoured

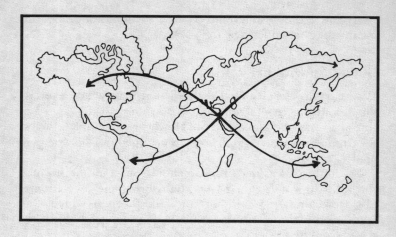

Out of Zion will shine the perfection of beauty.

in the sight of the Lord, and my God is my strength, He says, "It is too small a thing that you should be My servant to raise up the tribes of Jacob, and to restore the preserved ones of Israel; I will also make you a light of the nations so that My salvation may reach to the end of the earth."' (Isaiah 49:5–6 NASB)

Once more Isaiah, reflecting upon Israel's unique calling to be a light of God's revelation to the world, writes,

'... for the Lord has redeemed Jacob and in Israel He shows forth His glory ...' (Isaiah 44:23 NASB)

Paul, having well understood the particular calling that God gave to Israel, writes in Romans 9:1–5:

'... For I could wish that I myself were accursed, separated from Christ for the sake of my brethren, my kinsmen according to the flesh, who are Israelites, to whom belongs the adoption as sons and the glory and the covenants and the giving of the law and the temple service and the promises, whose are the fathers, and from whom is the Christ according to the flesh, who is over all, God blessed forever. Amen . . .'

Tolstoy, commenting on Israel's calling and servant relationship to the world, writes: 'The Jew is that sacred being who has brought down from heaven the everlasting fire and has illumined with it the entire world . . .' In his book, 'The Jew and Modern Israel', Milton Lindberg writes: 'On the pages of history the wisdom of God stands vindicated in the choice of the Jews, not only as those to whom He would reveal His own glorious character, but also as a channel of blessing and a vehicle for the transmission of the knowledge of God to the whole earth . . .'

Perhaps the easiet way to describe Israel's relationship to God and subsequent responsibility to the world is to say that Israel became God's private secretary!

However, this choice of Israel as God's 'servant nation' would have two serious consequences:

1. The survival of the human race would be bound up with the survival of the Jewish race, and
2. The destruction of Israel would become the devil's highest priority as in this way he would banish the revelation and knowledge of God from the face of the earth.

In short, the destruction of the Jewish race would mean the destruction of the human race. In a certain sense, therefore, Israel became the world's most precious possession! Leon Uris, the famous Jewish author and historian, writes: 'It is my personal belief that Zionism is a historical necessity. Israel is the object of much love and affection. But, above all, Israel is needed . . .' If only the world and the church would recognise this.

It is for this reason that God says He will bless those who bless her and curse those who curse her. To bless her is to work for the eternal survival of the human race, but to curse her is to work for the destruction of the human race!

To put it clearly: if Israel survives then ultimately the devil and his diabolical system will be destroyed. No one knows this better than the devil himself and thus he perceives Israel as his number one target. The result of all this and has been holocaust ... or the planned murder of the whole Jewish nation.

History clearly agrees with this. Pharoah, Haman, Titus and Hitler have all tried it and today the Russians and the Yassir Arafats of our world are seeking to attempt it.

Israel has become the most trampled upon, hated and persecuted nation that the world has ever known. W. W. Fereday, writing in 1919, long before the restoration of the Jewish state, said: 'Prophecy revolves around the despised Jew, and if Jewish restoration is imminent (as it appears to be), how near we must be to the fulfilment of every vision ...' Undoubtedly the devil knows 'that he has only a short time' and thus we can expect his anger against Israel to increase. Revelation 12 declares that he will persecute 'the woman' (Israel) with 'great Wrath' (Revelation 12:12 and 13).

Yes, truly the sufferings of Israel are bound up with her calling. E. A. Josephson quite rightly underlines the implications of this suffering when he points out that 'The Jews through the centuries have taken the full brunt of Satan's attacks for our sakes ...'

However, Israel's sufferings are also ...

Bound up with her destiny

The great responsibility that Israel accepted also meant that she would inherit great privileges. The privileges can be summarised as follows:

1. Those that are spiritual. To her was given the revelation of God's Word, the Prophets, the Covenants and the Messiah. See Romans 9:1–5 and John 4:22.
2. Those that are physical. To her was given the land as an everlasting possession ... ratified by the Abrahamic and Palestinian Covenants, and
3. Those that are regal. God has promised to exalt Israel as the chief nation in the earth. Isaiah, referring to this coming day, writes,

'Arise shine; for your light has come, and the glory of the Lord has risen upon you. For behold darkness will cover the earth and deep darkness the peoples; but the Lord will rise upon you. And the nations will come to your light, and kings to the brightness of your rising . . .'

(Isaiah 60:1–3 NASB)

See also Isaiah 2:1–4, Jeremiah 3:17 and Malachi 3:17.

This third privilege, in particular, has to do with her destiny and its fulfilment is dependent upon two things:

1. Her restoration to the land, and
2. Her restoration to the Lord through Messiah Jesus.

When these two restorations are achieved God has promised to send Jesus a second time, establish world peace and exalt Israel as a blessing in the midst of the earth. In other words, the conclusion of world redemption is dependent upon Israel's preservation, physical restoration and redemption. In this respect Acts 3:18–21 is worth noting:

'But the things which God announced before hand by the mouth of all the prophets, that His Christ should suffer, He has fulfilled. Repent therefore and return, that your sins may be wiped away in order that times of refreshing may come from the presence of the Lord, and that He may send Jesus, the Messiah appointed for you, Whom heaven must receive until the period of restoration of all things, about which God spoke by the mouth of His holy prophets from ancient time . . .'

It must be noted from this passage that Peter is addressing Jews and is clear about the fact that Jesus's second coming is dependent upon the 'restoration of all things' – that is, it is dependent upon Jewish acceptance of Jesus as Messiah. Indeed the rest of the passage only confirms that his subject is the Jews and their restoration.

Now, nobody knows this better than the devil and thus, as the Bible predicts, in order to prevent world peace he will

51

Jesus, the
offspring and
root of David.

constantly endeavour to destroy Israel, or, if he cannot
destroy Israel, he will delay her acceptance of Jesus as the
Messiah by using ignorant Christians and nominal Christians to speak evil and do evil against her in the name of
Jesus!

This is the sad record of 1800 years of Christian history –
the name that saves has been used to kill. For instance, a
German publication during the Second World War stated:
'In the person of the Fuhrer we behold the messenger sent by
God who brings Germany into the presence of the God of
history. There is only one option, the visible church must be

filled with the national socialist spirit. We German Christians are the inner line of national Socialism. To live, fight and die for Adolf Hitler means to say, "yes" to the way of Christ . . .'

This so-called Christian dedication to Adolf Hitler resulted in the planned murder of six million Jews. No wonder we have difficulty in convincing the Jews that Jesus is their Messiah!

E. A. Josephson is therefore right when he writes: 'The horrible irony is that Satan's emissaries have deceived the whole world with their "cloak and dagger" tactic, with Christ's cloak and the devil's dagger . . .'

How then, in the light of this diabolical reality, can we expect them to believe in the cross when for hundreds of years it has been used as a sword against them? In short, this has been the work of the devil to keep Israel from reaching her God-given destiny. The true peacemakers of the world are, therefore, those that labour for Israel's preservation, land restoration and conversion.

Only this will bring the 'Prince of Peace' back to establish 'A new world order' of peace and righteousness. Isaiah 62:6–7 states,

> 'On your walls, O Jerusalem, I have appointed watchmen, All day and all night they will never keep silent. You who remind the Lord, take no rest for yourselves, and give Him no rest until He establishes and makes Jerusalem a praise in the earth.'

God has a principle of . . .

> 'To the Jew first and then to the Gentile.' 'For you first, i.e. the Jew . . . God raised up His Servant, and sent Him to bless you by turning every one of you from your wicked ways . . .' (Acts 3:26 NASB)

Whilst unbelief in Israel has 'delayed' God's purposes for world peace it is still true that world peace will only come when she experiences peace first. This will only happen when

Jesus comes to the Mount of Olives a second time. Jesus Himself said this:

> 'And when He approached, He saw the city and wept over it, saying, "If you had known in this day, even you, the things which make for peace! But now they have been hidden from your eyes. For the days shall come upon you when your enemies will throw up a bank before you, and surround you, and hem you in on every side, and will level you to the ground and your children within you, and they will not leave in you one stone upon another, because you did not recognise the time of your visitation ..."' (Luke 19:41–44 NASB)

And

> 'O Jerusalem, Jerusalem, who kills the prophets and stones those who are sent to her! How often I wanted to gather your children together, the way a hen gathers her chicks under her wings, and you were unwilling. Behold, your house is being left to you desolate! For I say to you, from now on you shall not see Me until you say, "Blessed is He who comes in the name of the Lord".' (Matthew 23:37–39 NASB)

It will be noted from these verses that the Prince of Peace will only establish peace in the earth when Israel invites Him back to do so! The real United Nations of the world is thus Jerusalem. It is thus also no coincidence that when the Balfour Declaration of November 1917 opened the door for a restored Jewish homeland in Palestine, the powers of darkness engineered, in that same month and year, the birth of Israel's greatest enemy, Soviet Russia.

Of this nation Gaebelein once wrote: 'Bolshevism is the violence of the wicked aiming at God's order in government and the overthrow of everything ...'

Indeed the sufferings of Israel are bound up with her destiny. However, Israel's sufferings are also ...

Bound up with her rebellion

Israel's calling and destiny before God should in no way lead us into thinking that she is 'on the perfect side of being human.' No, a Jew has the same fallen nature as a Gentile.

However, Israel's peculiar standing before God, whilst giving her privileges, also gave her awesome responsibilities, namely, to be the people of God, to reflect Him to the world and to make His name great in the earth.

World redemption was dependent upon her faithfulness in these areas. Unfaithfulness would mean correction, judgment and chastisement.

Unfortunately, Israel has been stubborn and unfaithful, leaving God no other choice but to judge and correct her. Her two exiles are to be seen in this context.

Indeed the destruction of the temple prior to both exiles symbolised as it were, God's displeasure of her as it happened on exactly the same day on both occasions ... the ninth day of Av.

A passage of scripture adequately expressing God's corrective measures against Israel is that which is to be found in Jeremiah 30:10–11:

> '... And fear not, O Jacob My servant,' declares the Lord, 'And do not be dismayed, O Israel; for behold, I will save you from afar, and your offspring from the land of their captivity. And Jacob shall return, and shall be quiet and at ease, and no one shall make him afraid.
>
> For I am with you, declares the Lord, to save you: for I will destroy completely all the nations where I have scattered you, only I will not destroy you completely. But I will chasten you justly, and will by no means leave you unpunished ...'

Note also: Isaiah 1:2–4; Isaiah 48:10; Isaiah 54:7–8; Leviticus 26:14–46; Deuteronomy 32:15–33; 2 Chronicles 36:14 and Ezekiel 5:7–17.

Israel's own sin, disobedience and rebellion has thus contributed to her suffering. Yet the nations have sought to

'Who is so stubborn as my servant Israel?'

further God's judgment against Israel and for this they stand condemned before Him. In this respect Zechariah writes:

'So the angel who was speaking with me said to me, "Proclaim saying, Thus says the Lord of hosts, I am exceedingly jealous for Jerusalem and Zion. But I am very angry with the nations who are at ease: for while I was only a little angry, they furthered the disaster ...'
(Zechariah 1:14–15 NASB)

Chapter 4

The church and Israel

'And those who will walk by this rule, peace and mercy be upon them, and upon the Israel of God.'

(Gal. 6:16 NASB)

In Galatians 6:16, Paul refers to the believing church as the 'Israel of God' leading many to believe that the church has now replaced Israel, she being completely abandoned by God because of her unbelief.

But, did Paul really mean the 'replacement theory?' I think not. The fact that the church is called Israel in Galatians doesn't mean or imply replacement but rather enlargement and fulfilment. Indeed, if Paul meant replacement he would be contradicting everything that he wrote about the church and Israel in his epistles to the Romans and Ephesians.

For instance, in his epistle to the Romans, he speaks of the church, like a wild olive tree, being grafted into Israel, the natural olive tree. By the use of this analogy any thought of replacement becomes impossible as the text is clearly speaking about inclusion and enlargement!

'But, if some of the branches were broken off, and you, being a wild olive, were grafted in among them and became partakers with them of the rich root of the olive

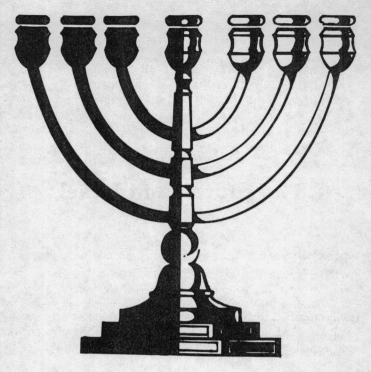

The 'Menorah' – a symbol of Israel and of the church.

tree, do not be arrogant toward the branches, but if you are arrogant, remember that it is not you who supports the root, but the root supports you.'

(Romans 11:17–18 NASB)

It is important for us to note the phrases that Paul employs in this passage ... phrases like 'grafted in', 'with them', 'do not be arrogant', and 'the root supports you'. All these phrases should steer us completely away from any 'replacement theory'. Unfortunately, church history affirms that many spiritual leaders failed to take this exhortation and warning, resulting in arrogance toward unbelieving Israel and, in some cases, anti-Semitism.

Paul's theology in Ephesians is exactly the same as, in

chapter two of this great epistle, he speaks of the church as being included in the commonwealth of Israel.

> 'Therefore remember, that formerly you, the Gentiles in the flesh, who are called "Uncircumcision" by the so-called "Circumcision" which is performed in the flesh by human hands – remember that you were at that time separate from Christ, excluded from the commonwealth of Israel, and strangers to the covenants of promise, having no hope and without God in the world.
>
> 'But now in Christ Jesus you who formerly were far off have been brought near by the blood of Christ.'
>
> (Ephesians 2:11–13 NASB)

Again it is important for us to note that his theology is not the church replacing Israel but rather the church being included in Israel. To use Paul's words, we 'have been brought near' ... to the commonwealth of Israel. How then do we define this 'brought near' or 'grafted in' theology of Paul's? Or, to put it more simply, what is the present relationship between the church and Israel? The answer to this important question lies in ...

Understanding the family

The church and Israel, though distinct, nevertheless belong to the same family. The fact that the church is 'grafted in' can only imply this. This relationship between the church and Israel may be described in terms of a parent and son. Both are distinct but nevertheless enjoy the same name and privileges. In our analogy, the parent – Israel – represents the source and as such is localised. Hence Israel was established in Canaan or Palestine in order to father or give birth to the revelation and people of God. For her the land, which binds them together forever, is essential. This eternal bond with 'the land' is expressed each passover by Jews everywhere when they say, 'next year in Jerusalem'.

Elian J. Finbert, commenting on this amazing bond between the Jew and Canaan, writes: 'Such has been their

59

power of visionary substitution that, in their minds, they have never left the soil but have gone on cultivating it, ploughing, irrigating, weeding.' Years before the restoration of the Jewish state, Disraeli remarked: 'The vineyards of Israel are no more, but the eternal law enjoins upon the sons of Israel to celebrate the grape-harvest. A race which persists in celebrating the grape-harvest despite having not grapes to gather will have its vineyards again ...' And we might add, 'And so she did!'

The son, on the other hand, being the church, represents the fruit or the fulfilment of Divine promise. As such, the son is delocalised. That is, whilst the parent stays in the home forever it is the children that leave and 'spread their wings'. Thus the church had her birth in Jerusalem but subsequently went to the ends of the earth. However, without a parent there is no son and so the son owes his life to the parent who brought him into the world.

The church would therefore do well to remember that her origins are entirely Jewish. In fact, it was because of the death of a Jew that she received the gift of eternal life! J. Verkuyl, expressing this important truth in his book, 'Contemporary Missiology', writes: 'Let every Christian remind himself that the synagogue is the mother of the church and that we Gentiles need the Jews lest we fall back into the "ways" of the heathen ...'

The difference, then, between the church and Israel is not origin but function. The basic function of Israel is to birth truth. However, the basic function of the son or the church is to gather all nations into the truth, or ... into the family. Function does not imply inequality, but role. The church is not inferior to Israel the parent. No, she is simply distinct though dependent. Paul says: 'The root supports you'. (Romans 11:18)

When Jesus comes a second time, as with parents and sons, there will be a family reunion. We the church will meet our Godly fathers who constitute the source and roots of our faith and she, Israel, having the veil of blindness taken from her eyes, will recognise her sons, as many as the stars of the sky and as the sand upon the seashore. These sons constitute

Israel's fruitfulness and they will be a living testimony to God's faithfulness to her. Thus even in eternity our functions will be different – their full nature and extent are not as yet revealed – but we shall be one happy family!

Indeed a casual glance at Revelation 21–22 reveals that parent and son will one day in eternity occupy the same dwelling again – the New Jerusalem. Speaking of this city John writes:

> 'It had a great and high wall, with twelve gates, and at the gates twelve angels; and names were written on them, which are those of the twelve tribes of Israel ...' and '... the wall of the city had twelve foundation stones and on them were the twelve names of the twelve apostles of the Lamb ...' (Revelation 21:12,14 NASB)

Though scripture looks forward to a day of harmony in the family, present history unfortunately bears testimony to ...

A family squabble between father and son

The parent Israel has become blind, not recognising his fruit and the joy thereof ... and the son, being the church, has become stunted or underdeveloped not recognising the wealth of wisdom and the storehouse of knowledge that is resident in the father's house!

However, we are beginning to see the dawning of a new day, for God the Holy Spirit is opening our spiritual eyes to behold these things. The church is again discovering her Jewish roots and Israel is beginning to recognise the life and vitality of the church.

All this is precisely what Paul has to say in Romans 11 where throughout the chapter he uses the analogy of a tree with its branches. The tree with its branches symbolises Israel and the church. They belong together! The tree with its uprooted Israel and the branches represent the church. Branches spread out and run but the trunk remains secure in its soil. Both are distinct but belong nevertheless to the same tree.

The age-old conflict between the church and Israel.

Roots require soil – so Israel needs the land, and branches require space, so the church can fill the world but both require each other. May God the Holy Spirit help us to see our mutual interdependence. Indeed the anti-God left-wing media of our world are already discerning this mutual relationship between Israel and the church as they have been attacking what they call the Judeo-Christian ethic.

In Russia, Jews and Christians are presently suffering together. I have no doubt that God is bringing the two 'groups' together in such a way that we the church will abandon our arrogance and care for Israel, and Israel will abandon her unbelief and welcome the church into the family – the Israel of God.

Scripture agrees with this as Paul writes:

> 'For I do not want you, brethren, to be uninformed of this mystery, lest you be wise in your own estimation, that a partial hardening has happened to Israel until the fullness of the Gentiles has come in: and thus all Israel (the church and the nation) will be saved ...'
>
> (Romans 11:25–26 NASB)

In the interest of clarity

In bringing this chapter to a close it may be good for us to pass some comment about the passages in the New Testament which refer to the fact that there is neither Jew nor Gentile in the church but one new man. In this respect note Galatians 3:28:

> 'There is neither Jew nor Greek, there is neither slave nor free man, there is neither male nor female, for you are all one in Christ Jesus ...'

Such passages as the above are often used to bolster the argument that sees the church as everything and Israel as nothing.

The fact is, however, that in these passages the apostle Paul is not teaching about the church or Israel but rather about the dismantling of prejudice and hatred that has kept these two entities or realities apart. This hatred and prejudice is done away with in Christ. Furthermore it will be noted that the passage referred to here from Galatians goes on to declare that in Christ there is also neither male nor

Let us clarify the issues ...

female. Are we then to believe that when one comes to Christ one undergoes a sex change! Obviously not. Male remains male and female remains female just as Israel remains Israel and the church remains the church. However, the prejudice and resentment between these groups is torn down.

In fact, in Christ all prejudice and hatred between all men should be dismantled. Black men remain black men and white men remain white, but in Christ the enmity between them should go. Indeed, as Paul affirms, in the first chapter of Romans, racial, cultural, sexual and intellectual barriers must go by virtue of our being in Christ (Romans 1:14–16).

The reason is simple: we've all joined the same family – the family of God. Or, to use the correct family name, Israel.

Finally, getting back to our father-son analogy. A father is duty bound to lay down his life for his children. History affirms that this is exactly what happened. Jewish prophets, teachers, evangelists, apostles and a Jewish Messiah laid down their lives in order to bring us the saving gospel and, with it, eternal life. However, there comes a time in every family when the sons have to lay down their lives for their father in order to care for and protect him.

I believe that the church, being 'the son', is now being called upon to pay her debt to Israel, the father. Let us not be slothful in doing so. Let us rise up to love, help and comfort Zion.

> 'Comfort, O comfort My people,' says your God. 'Speak kindly to Jerusalem, and call out to her that her warfare has ended. That her iniquity has been removed, that she has received of the Lord's hand double for all her sins . . .' (Isaiah 40:1 NASB)

The gospel –
'to the Jew first and also to the Greek.'

Chapter 5

Mission and Israel

'And he said to them, Go into all the world and preach the gospel to all creation.'

(Mark 16:15 NASB)

The church, by virtue of her mandate, must be missionary minded. Her task is to preach the gospel to every creature. No group, nation or community is exempt from the church's missionary thrust. For the church to make such an exemption would mean placing herself in a position of disobedience to the command of Jesus. Our missionary strategy must, therefore, include Israel. In fact, the scriptures affirm that the gospel is for the Jew first.

> 'For I am not ashamed of the gospel, for it is the power of God for salvation to everyone who believes, to the Jew first and also to the Greek ...' (Romans 1:16 NASB)

As servants of Messiah Jesus we must thus be fully committed to the evangelisation of the Jewish nation. However, the way in which this is done is the all-important question for us to answer. There are those who favour the 'direct method' of approach. That is, to challenge the Jewish community openly and directly about their attitude towards Jesus of Nazareth. However, there are others, like the author, who regard the direct approach as being misguided and prefer rather to approach them with due consideration of the serious historical problems. In fact, it is no secret that the 'direct method' has, up until now, yielded very little positive fruit. The reason for this is clear . . .

A problem of credibility

As Christians our historical dealings with the Jews have been deplorable. Our previous chapters have dealt with this problem at some length and thus I shall not enlarge on it here. However, let us clearly understand that to 'buttonhole' Jews and call upon them to repent and accept Christ without considering the problems of our history is like letting thieves and drunkards propagate the gospel from our pulpits. Such would be stumbling blocks to faith in Jesus, and our history is a terrible stumbling block to the Jewish nation.

In short, the time has come for us to earn the right to speak. J. Verkuyl, in his book, 'Contemporary Missiology', writes the following, concerning the Christian response to Jews after the Second World War: 'Christians began to realise that it was precisely they who for a significant portion of their history had caused the Jews so much agony and left a deep scar on their collective consciousness. European Christians had previously wiped clean their own memories of these deeds. But not any longer. What happened during the Second World War has so seared Christians' consciences and opened their eyes to the past that any meeting between Jew and Christian cannot evade this issue . . .'

Again, considering Christian Jewish relationships throughout history, Verkuyl says: 'In all honesty and candour the Christian church must admit that the history of her contact with Jews is a shameful one . . .'

Those who find it in their hearts to deny this conclusion have simply never taken the time to read history books. Their objection is therefore couched in ignorance.

In the light of all this, it must be concluded that we have a serious credibility problem. This in turn means that we have a lot of work to do in the area of the 'proclamation of our lives.'

The church's testimony lies in ruins.

A Communist once climbed onto his soap box in Hyde Park and began to declare the virtues, as he saw them, of Communism. However, at a certain point in his speech, when he took a breath, a bystander quickly seized his opportunity and cried out, 'Your life speaks so loudly that I can't hear what you're saying ...'

This little episode adequately sums up the present Jewish response to our verbal proclamation of the gospel. It is important for us to know this.

Looking to the future

In the light of our credibility problem, our contact with the Jewish community ought to be governed by a number of vital principles. The first of these is ...

1. That of unconditional love

For too long Christian interest in the Jews has been regulated by their response to our missionary overtures. If these overtures have been rejected then the interest has been withdrawn, and in many cases replaced with antagonism and even anti-Semitism.

Such was the case with Martin Luther. Initially, he was deeply interested in the Jewish community and even made a lot of friends amongst them. However, when that community rejected his evangelistic endeavours, he quickly turned against them. In this respect, J. Verkuyl writes: 'One can detect two phases in Luther's attitude. Prompted by a missionary spirit, Luther initially expressed an interest in the Jews, but later, having been disappointed in their response, his love turned to fierce rejection ...'

This conditional love attitude towards the Jews is not something peculiar to Luther. Indeed, it has been the general Christian attitude throughout history. In the light of scripture it is untenable and inexcusable as, in spite of their rejection of Jesus as Messiah, the New Testament still affirms that God loves them:

'From the standpoint of the gospel they are enemies for

70

your sake, but from the standpoint of God's choice they are beloved for the sake of the fathers.'   (Romans 11:28)

Moreover, more than any other group in the world we, as Christians, should be committed to unconditional love in our relationships with our fellow men as we ourselves have been recipients of such love in Christ Jesus. In this connection scripture declares:

> 'But God demonstrates His own love toward us, in that while we were yet sinners, Christ died for us ...'
>
> (Romans 5:8 NASB)

2.   The ministry of comfort

Jewish history has been a suffering one. In fact, their sufferings have no parallel in any other nation. Even if part of this suffering has been because of their own rebellion, it is not for us as Christian people to have any part of it.

'Vengeance is mine, says the Lord' (Deut. 32:35) and as such it remains forever and always a divine prerogative and pre-occupation only!

If we have any responsibility at all it is to comfort and care for God's suffering ancient people:

> 'Comfort, O comfort My people,' says your God. 'Speak kindly to Jerusalem, and call out to her, that her warfare has ended, that her iniquity has been removed, that she has received of the Lord's hand double for all her sins ...'
>
> (Isaiah 40:1–2 NASB)

Such comfort must be meaningful, practical and sacrificial. In this context the work of the International Christian Embassy in Jerusalem is particularly valuable as the Embassy is supportive of many social and rehabilitative programmes in Israel. In this way real Christian love and comfort is being demonstrated.

In addition Christians have, in recent years, fully involved themselves in the Soviet Jewry campaign. Their involvement in this pressing issue has made a positive contribution to the worldwide call for the release of many refuseniks and prisoners of Zion.

Apart from these high profile activities there are many other ways in which Christians can comfort Israel. Perhaps one of the most meaningful ways in which this can be done is to befriend Jews in our community. Such befriending should be sincere and genuine and it should be characterised by an acceptance of the Jews as they are. Above all, any Christian wishing to comfort Israel should at least do a little reading about Jewish history and tradition beforehand. This will enable the Christian to appreciate the difficulties and problems that have always clouded Jewish-Christian relationships. Also, it will enable the Christian to understand why they are so extremely sensitive to certain subjects, such as missionary activity.

The third principle governing Christian Jewish contact should be ...

3. *The importance of dialogue*

In the light of all that we have said so far, it is clear that the traditional forms of evangelism have to give way to a more credible, life-based form of evangelism when dealing with the Jewish community.

Indeed, this is precisely what the Word of God teaches as it calls upon us to live out our Christian testimony before the Jewish community that they are provoked to jealousy.

> 'I say then they did not stumble so as to fall, did they? May it never be! But by their transgression, salvation has come to the Gentiles, to make them jealous ...'
>
> (Romans 11:11 NASB)

In short, our responsibility before God is to harmonise our talk with our walk. Talking of Jewish evangelism, a well-known Jewish Christian and author, Jacob Jocz, writes: 'There is but one way to proclaim the gospel and that is by living it ...'

Yet in all this, our verbal testimony is important and it is the author's convinced opinion that such verbal testimony should take place within the framework of sincere dialogue. Such dialogue, apart from being sincere, should also transpire in an atmosphere that is free from any 'buttonhole' pressure and it should provide an opportunity for each side to clearly state their feelings, fears and even objections. It should also leave us free to agree to disagree!

In this respect Louis Goldberg, a practising Jew, writes: 'We are reaching the point where we can talk to each other clearly, loyal to ourselves, but without hatred. Indeed, we do agree to disagree on key issues. It is clear that Jesus Christ is between Jews and Christians a stumbling block ...'

Quite obviously then, the central area of disagreement between Jews and Christians is that which has to do with Jesus of Nazareth and, in particular, His identity. However, this in no way means that He cannot be discussed. In fact, more than ever before Jesus has become the object of much discussion and examination by Jewish scholars. It is certainly not wrong to say that much of this scholarship considers Jesus to have been a great prophet and man of God.

For instance, a Jewish scholar from the Hebrew university in Jerusalem once said: 'I wish to remind my readers of one thing: the fact that Jesus both lived and died as a good Jew ought to fill every last one of us with pride ...'

And Dr Isodore Singer, the editor of the Jewish Encyclopedia, writes: 'I regard Jesus of Nazareth as a Jew of Jews, one whom all Jewish people are learning to love. His teachings have been an immense service in the world in bringing Israel's God to the knowledge of hundreds of millions of mankind.'

Finally, Ferdynand Zweig, in his work, 'The Figure of Jesus On The Israeli Horizon', writes: 'In the Diaspora Jesus looked alien to the Jew, an outsider, an interloper. But in Israel he is seen as the Jew from Nazareth, a native of this country, a Sabra, with claims to the land as strong as any. He cannot be brushed aside as a foreign influence ...'

Yes, indeed, I have known Jews to be more than ready to discuss Jesus once they have been assured of our friendship and genuine love. Moreover, I have no doubt that, if more honest, open dialogue took place between Jews and

Christians, we Christians would soon discover that we have a lot to learn from them about the very Bible we love and study!

They have a 'root' insight into and knowledge of the Word of God that opens up certain passages in such a way that they take on a clarity that we never thought possible or saw before. For this reason it is important that we as Christians should enter into such dialogue with a humble and teachable heart.

Verkuyl says: 'When we Christians enter the schoolhouse of Judaism we would do well to be modest and attentive.'

These, then, are the three crucial principles that should govern or regulate Christian mission to the Jewish community.

Above all, let our love for Jesus' brethren be so fervent and real that we reach out to them for Zion's sake!

Part Two

Devotional

Foreword

In this world there are only two communities of people with whom God has made specific and eternal covenants. They are the true and elect church of God, constituted by all who are born of His Spirit and the elect descendants of Abraham through Isaac and Jacob – Israel and Jewish people. The key to the divine purpose for the future ages is to be found in these two covenant peoples. Ultimately God will fuse them into one in that day when the knowledge of His glory will cover the earth as the waters cover the sea.

Sadly, over the years these two peoples have been progressively alienated by huge walls of suspicion, distrust and even hatred. Although some Christians find it hard to accept as truth, it is an historic fact that for the church's part she has not only devalued, ridiculed and misrepresented the Jew, but inspired much of the persecution, injustice and murder which has left Jewish history soaked with innocent blood. Instead of being a channel of divine love and blessing to them, she has cursed them. The time is long overdue for that kind of evil and wrong to be redressed.

For this reason I welcome this book by my dear friend, Malcolm Hedding. It represents and expresses a new attitude toward the Jew. I am especially glad that his main emphasis is a call to prayer for Israel and the Jewish people, for this has been a burden of mine for many years. It has so often been the case that any understanding of Israel's place in God's purpose for the nations has been seen only as evidence of the trustworthiness of His Word and as an encouragement to the faith of the Christian. Such an understanding has seldom ignited the Christian heart with love for the Jew, producing an enduring burden of intercession for them.

In acts of God written in modern history, we have witnessed the return of the Jew from the ends of earth to the promised land; the rebirth of Israel in the recreation of the Jewish State on the 14th May 1948; the reunification of Jerusalem on 6th and 7th June 1967; and Israel's miraculous preservation through five wars during the 39 years of her modern history, three of which could have spelt her liquidation. She now faces even greater problems and much greater acts of God as she moves into the last phases of world history.

God's call to the child of God to pray for Israel and the Jewish people until His purpose for them and for His church be fulfilled constitutes the challenge of this book. May it call forth a response from every reader.

Lance Lambert
Jerusalem
June 1987

Chapter 6

Who?

*'When you pray, go into your room, close the door and pray to
your Father, who is unseen ...'*   *(Matthew 6:6 NASB)*

A good deal of Christian support for Israel is fanciful, couched in misguided zeal, highly romanticised and, in the long
run, of little real value. While Israel is, of course, in need of
friends (and we should do everything to broaden this circle),
nevertheless our greatest act of friendship for Israel is that
which must and should take place in the prayer closet.

Daniel the prophet

This, surely, is the abiding lesson from the life of the prophet
Daniel who lived in the sixth century before Jesus, the
Messiah.

Daniel lived in a day when Israel was in exile in Babylon.
Her cities, in the land of promise, lay in ruins as did her
temple and national institutions. The Judgment of God had
finally caught up with her, and the prophet Daniel, acutely
aware of his people's sin, lamented this awful tragedy that
had befallen them (Daniel 9).

However, in response to a divine promise of restoration
tucked away in the oracle of the prophet Jeremiah, Daniel

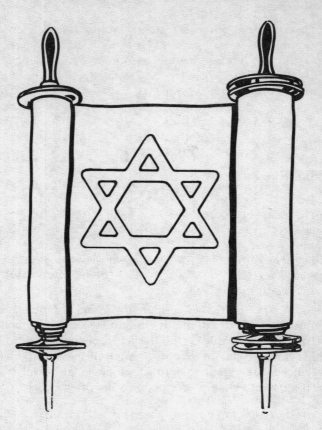

Tucked away in the oracle of the prophet Jeremiah.

found his heart strangely stirred. Not in a way that caused him to get up and found a new organisation, but, rather, in a way that led him to the place of believing prayer.

He determined in his heart to lay hold of the God of Heaven and thus to so call upon His name that He would be entreated to restore the fortunes of His people Israel.

Well, history alone testifies to the effectual nature of Daniel's prayers; for, in response to his prayerful cry, God not only initiated the programme that brought about Israel's

80

return to Canaan and full restoration, but He also revealed the destinies of great and mighty nations, right up until the end of time; that is, the consummation of the present age.

In short, Daniel's prayers are still affecting the lives of countless millions today! This, in itself, is a powerful testimony to the dramatic influence that sincere prayer can have upon our world and its history.

A man like us

Moreover, it must be remembered that Daniel was no 'superman' or 'angelic being'. No, he was nothing of the sort. He was merely a man like us, yet a dedicated believer in the God of Israel.

His life was prone to the same weaknesses and failures as ours, and, no doubt, he found himself frequently 'tripped up' by the depravity of his fallen nature – just as we are!

Yet his heart burned with a love for God and all his longings or desires were directed towards righteousness and Godly behaviour. This man prayed for Israel and did more for her than ten thousand organisations! Not that organisations are unimportant – they are important as we need some vehicle by which we can, in real physical terms, express our love for Israel. However, believing prayer is still more important and sometimes the proliferation of organisations, set up to bless and help Israel, cause us to think that our spiritual duty has been accomplished.

The truth is, Israel needs men and women, like Daniel, who will regularly pray for her. The ministry of prayer is just as powerful today as it was in that of Daniel's and Scripture affirms that God is a rewarder of them that diligently seek Him (Hebrews 11:6).

Moreover, as in Daniel's case, and for that matter, Elijah's, God is not looking for spiritual giants to be involved in this urgent matter. NO! He simply wants sincere, down-to-earth, blood-washed Christians. Indeed Hebrews 10:19–25 outlines the type of person that God, the Holy Spirit, is looking for:

'Therefore, brothers, since we have confidence to enter the Most Holy Place by the blood of Jesus, by a new and living way, opened for us through the curtain, that is His Body, and since we have a Great Priest over the house of God, let us draw near to God with a sincere heart in full assurance of faith, having our hearts sprinkled to cleanse us from a guilty conscience and having our bodies washed with pure water. Let us hold unswervingly to the hope we profess, for He who promised is faithful. And let us consider how we may spur one another on toward love and good deeds. Let us not give up meeting together, as some are in the habit of doing, but let us encourage one another – and all the more as you see the Day approaching.'

From this passage, we learn that the type of person that God is looking for is:

- A person of sincere heart;
- A person of believing heart;
- A person of righteous behaviour;
- A person of people interest; and
- A person of commitment to the Body of Christ.

Now, such a person, be he John, Allan, Jane, Mary, Daniel or Elijah, will change our world and in particular, do much for Israel through prayer.

Terrifying prayer jargon!

Sometimes folk who would willingly and eagerly give themselves to prayer for Israel are deterred, and even infused with a spiritual inferiority complex, because of the 'high sounding' spiritual terminology that some praying Christians insist on using ... phrases like, 'doing spiritual conflict', 'groaning in the Spirit', 'agonising in prayer', 'standing in the gap' and even the use of the word 'intercession'. My personal experience is that much of this language is simply 'hot air' and more often than not used to impress, rather than to indicate anything of real significance.

In short, forget it and ignore it! Note:

Prayer is simply talking to God ...

> **Prayer is simply talking to God in the light of what He has promised to do in His Word.**

This is all that Daniel did – nothing more and nothing less! This is all that God wants you to be doing! As we have different personalities, so we respond to the 'emotion' of prayer differently. Some folk tend to cry, others groan while yet others screw themselves up into the most uncomfortable physical positions. Still others are very quiet and show no outward emotion at all. All this is well and good but none of it makes us spiritual or our prayers more effective! Moreover, none of it constitutes a norm or standard for praying.

Jesus prayed in the Garden of Gethsemane and His intensity of heart became so great that He began to sweat great drops of blood. This was merely a consequence of the spiritual energy that was consuming His soul. It was in no way a requirement for sincere prayer and, as we all well know, He never, in all His teaching, suggested that it was.

In fact, Jesus' teaching about prayer was refreshingly simple in that it highlighted the fact that prayer is nothing more than a sincere conversation with God! His teaching had more to do with consistency, perseverance and honesty than it did with clichés and outward forms of intensity.

Indeed, for Jesus, spiritual jargon and outward form were things to be most often regarded with suspicion. Note: Matthew 6:7–8, Matthew 23:14.

So, then, you too can change history through your simple yet sincere prayers. Moreover, in praying for Israel you will be bringing the DAY OF WORLD PEACE AND REDEMPTION closer. In short, 'For The World's Sake', pray for Israel.

Chapter 7

Why?

'Pray for the peace of Jerusalem: May they prosper who love you ...'   *(Psalm 122:6 NASB)*

Most Christians live in countries far removed from Israel. In many cases their Christianity is so 'localised' that praying for Israel seems strange and unusual, to say the least.

In many countries Christianity has so drifted from its original Jewish roots that the thought that it has something to do with Israel also seems ridiculous. So, when we suggest that fervent and regular prayer should be offered up on behalf of God's ancient people the question that immediately arises in the hearts of people is, 'why?'

The answers to this are the following:

1.   Because the Word of God commands it

The Psalmist declared, 'Pray for the peace of Jerusalem'. This is a command and, in itself, should be sufficient motivation for us to pray regularly for Israel. However, prayer, while most certainly being an act of obedience, should also be intelligent. Jesus exhorts us in the Gospels to 'watch and pray'. That is, we are to keep abreast with that which is happening around us and our prayers are to be uttered in the light of these day-to-day 'happenings'. In this way we become relevant and we become truly the 'salt of the earth'. It will be good for us to remember that the mystery of prayer is this:

> **God in His sovereignty intervenes in the affairs of men because of the prayers of His people on earth!**

No better example of this can be found than that which is given to us in Revelation 8:1–5 NIV:

> 'When he opened the seventh seal, there was silence in heaven for about half an hour. And I saw the seven angels who stand before God, and to them were given seven trumpets. Another angel, who had a golden censer, came and stood at the altar. He was given much incense to offer, with the prayers of all the saints, on the golden altar before the throne.
>
> The smoke of the incense, together with the prayers of the saints, went up before God from the angel's hand. Then the angel took the censer, filled it with fire from the altar, and hurled it on the earth; and there came peals of thunder, rumblings, flashes of lightning and an earthquake . . .'

In this passage, God's acts of judgment are clearly attributed to the prayers of His people on earth. Such prayer rises as incense before Him and moves Him to intervene in the affairs of men.

In fact, it is to be noted that so highly does God regard the faithful prayers of His people, that all of heaven comes to a reverent standstill, for half an hour, in honour of them! The message is clear: prayer moves heaven, changes the condition of men and has eternal consequences. This should surely encourage us as we obediently pray for the PEACE OF JERUSALEM.

2. Because world redemption is linked to Israel's redemption

As Christian people we talk much about the 'veil of unbelief' that lies over the hearts and minds of God's ancient people. However, many Christians, perhaps the majority, fail to understand the unique position that the Nation of Israel occupies in God's plan for world redemption. This is so in spite of the clear teaching of God's Word in this regard, especially in the New Testament. There is a veil of ignorance over their minds and understanding!

In short, the Word of God teaches that Jesus' second coming will not take place until Israel is redeemed and invites Him back to be their King.

The splitting of the veil brought about a new dispensation.

'O Jerusalem, Jerusalem, you who kill the prophets and stone those sent to you, how often I have longed to gather your children together, as a hen gathers her chicks under her wings, but you were not willing. Look, your house is left to you desolate. For I tell you, you will not see me again until you say, "Blessed is He who comes in the name of the Lord" ...'

(Matthew 23:37–39 NIV)

In Paul's Epistle to the Romans he makes the same point in chapter eleven and verses 25 to 27. Here Israel's salvation ushers in the coming of the deliverer 'from Zion', that is, the Lord Jesus Christ.

'... Israel has experienced a hardening in part until the full number of the Gentiles has come in. And so all Israel will be saved, as it is written:
    'The Deliverer will come from Zion; He will turn godlessness away from Jacob ...'

Naturally, according to all the prophets, the second coming of Jesus also ushers in world peace. That is, the time when men shall no longer learn war but, instead 'Beat their swords into plowshares and their spears into pruning hooks ...' (Isaiah 2:4)

This glorious day of peace, safety and Messiah's reign will only be ushered in when Israel turns from her unbelief and accepts and welcomes her Messiah, Jesus. The truth is, Israel's unbelief is the only hindrance to world peace. Only prayer will tear down this 'barrier' and pave the way for Jesus' second coming.

> **Anybody, therefore, who longs for the second coming of Jesus will bring it closer by being consumed with a fervent desire to pray for Israel. (II Peter 3:11–12)**

Israel, then, is the key to world redemption. This is precisely why scripture declares that we are not to give God any rest until He establishes Jerusalem as a praise in the earth:

> 'On your walls, O Jerusalem, I have appointed watchmen; all day and all night they will not keep silent. You who remind the Lord, take no rest for yourselves; and give Him no rest until He establishes and makes Jerusalem a praise in the earth.'   (Isaiah 62:6–7 NASB)

Yes, surely, the veil of ignorance needs to be lifted from the hearts and minds of Gentile believers in Jesus the Messiah. Any view of the second coming of Jesus for the church that excludes the redemption of Israel is a failure to appreciate the special place that Israel occupies in God's economy for the world. Paul said that we are to be careful that such ignorance, arrogance and conceit should not overtake us. When it does, we are hindered from effectively praying in the establishment of God's Kingdom on earth (Romans 11:20–21,25 Romans 10:1).

3.   Because we are debtors to Israel

In Romans 15:27 we read:

> '... for if the Gentiles have shared in the Jews' spiritual blessings, they owe it to the Jews to share with them their material blessings.'

Here Paul is not so much concerned with the 'means of blessing', which in this case happened to be material by nature, but, rather, in order to promote or motivate the giving of such means he underlines a principle, namely: that we are indebted to Israel.

Every Christian who enjoys a personal relationship with the God of heaven does so because of the faithfulness of God's people, Israel. They gave this knowledge to the world through their Book, their prophets, their apostles and their Messiah. Often they did this at great personal risk and many of them were martyred because of the 'eternal fire' that burned in their hearts. Indeed, tradition tells us that ten of the twelve apostles died violent deaths!

Yes, we are debtors to Israel and the time has surely come for us to pay back this debt. The most effective way in which we can do this is by praying for their salvation, redemption and eternal peace!

4. Because we are part of Israel

The Person we love and adore the most is a Jew. In fact He comes from the tribe of Judah, according to the flesh!

> Then one of the elders said to me, 'Do not weep! See, the Lion of the tribe of Judah, the Root of David, has triumphed. He is able to open the scroll and the seven seals . . .'
> (Revelation 5:5 NASB)

We cannot love Him and ignore His people Israel – He will not let us! He wept over His people, and He still does, and those who love Him must surely share that which is close to His heart? In fact, scripture affirms that His burdens are to become ours (Matthew 11:29–30). In this way we become an extension of His love in the world.

Moreover, Paul said that the church has not replaced Israel but rather she has been included in her commonwealth:

> '. . . remember that you were at that time separate from Christ, excluded from the commonwealth of Israel, and strangers to the covenants of promise, having no hope and without God in the world. But now in Christ Jesus you who formerly were far off have been brought near by the blood of Christ.'
> (Ephesians 2:12–13 NIV)

In his epistle to the Romans he employs many words and phrases in chapter eleven to bring this point home to the church. Phrases like, 'The church has been grafted into Israel' (verse 17), 'The church is supported by a Jewish root'

We cannot love him and ignore His people Israel.

(verse 18) and, 'You were cut out of an olive tree that is wild by nature, and, contrary to nature were grafted into a cultivated olive tree (Israel)' (verse 24).

So, it is clear that every born-again Christian should have a spontaneous love and concern for Israel. This is the testimony of many, including the author. My love and concern for Israel came about solely because of my commitment to Jesus, the Messiah.

The nature of the tree is determined by the root. I can well recall my early childhood days when my father would plant various shrubs, trees and bushes in our garden. Some of these were merely root systems and yet they grew to be distinctive, beautiful trees. The branches were the visible evidence of the same life beneath the ground.

Scripture affirms that we come from a Jewish root. There-fore, being 'grafted-in' branches, we should have in our hearts a feeling of belonging to Israel – or, if you like, a 'beneath the ground' feeling of belonging! This 'belonging' should drive us to the place of prayer for Israel. Such prayer has more to do with origin than with theology. In short, since we belong to the same tree, there should be a natural feeling of affinity, expressing itself in believing prayer.

5. Because we are commanded to pray for all men

Such is the command of scripture:

> 'I urge, then, first of all, that requests, prayers, interces-sion and thanksgiving be made for everyone – for kings and all those in authority, that we may live peaceful and quiet lives in all godliness and holiness. This is good, and pleases God our Saviour, who wants all men to be saved and to come to a knowledge of the truth ...'
>
> (I Timothy 2:1–4 NIV)

Since all have become partakers of Adam's evil nature all are in need of Christ's redemption, including Israel. Paul wrote:

> 'Brothers, my heart's desire and prayer to God for the Israelites is that they may be saved ...'
>
> (Romans 10:1 NIV)

In many ways, prayer is one of the supreme acts of love, as it brings those in need to the throne of God, the supreme power in the universe. In addition, one's earnest desire for the good and blessing of others, expressed through intercession, can lead one to a place of desired self-destruction so that others might live! As Paul considered the plight of his nation Israel, he wrote:

> 'For I could wish that I myself were cursed and cut off from Christ for the sake of my brothers, those of my own race, the people of Israel ...'   (Romans 9:3 NIV)

The supreme act of sacrificial prayer, brought into harmony with the Supreme Power, will have redemptive results in our world. Blessed are those who dedicate their lives to such a holy work. However, more blessed is he who is prayed for in this way. Let us rise up and do so for Jacob!

God is a prayer-answering God, and, though many may scoff at the worth of prayer, we who believe know that there is nothing more powerful on the face of the earth.

I have often been comforted and strengthened by the fact that I know that many have prayed, and do pray, for me. Indeed, in a way that defies human explanation, I have frequently felt the impact and 'lifting power' of such prayers. Surely, if thousands of Christians the world over begin to pray for Israel the dramatic and eternal effect upon this crucial nation will be great!

6. Because we shall prosper if we pray for Israel

'Pray for the peace of Jerusalem: May they prosper who love you.'

This is the promise of Psalm 122:6. God always blesses those who understand His purposes and flow with them. However, too many are so distant from God's heart that they cannot appreciate the important place that Israel occupies in His plan for the world.

God's blessings are always given to those who 'pay the price' in spite of being misunderstood by their brethren. It must be noted that many in the church consider concern and love for Israel to be misguided. God nevertheless promises to 'prosper' those who pray for Jerusalem.

These 'prospering blessings' are not to be understood as being merely physical or material by nature – but, rather, as those which give us greater understanding and insight into the purposes of God for our day.

Abraham walked in the purposes of God in that he obeyed, even though he did not know where such obedience would lead him (Hebrews 11:8). His reward was a special friendship with God that allowed him to share in God's thoughts and

We can't wash our hands!

intentions (Genesis 18:17–19). For the dedicated child of God, nothing could prosper him more than to share in this unique privilege.

Scripture affirms that they who know their God shall rise up and do exploits (Daniel 11:32). The 'exploits' are dependent upon the knowledge that we have of God and His purposes. Blessed is the man that is so situated – surely he is prospering!

We shall also prosper in this way if we understand the importance of Israel and pray regularly for her. Praying for Israel is praying for world peace. In short, in praying for Israel you are praying for the world's survival! Are we sufficient for these things? 'For the World's Sake' may we rise to such a challenge.

Chapter 8

When?

'First of all, then, I urge that entreaties and prayers, petitions and thanksgivings, be made on behalf of all men, for kings and all who are in authority, in order that we may lead a tranquil and quiet life in all godliness and dignity.' (I Timothy 2:1–2 NASB)

The subject of prayer is a vast one as there are many types of prayers that can be prayed. Scripture speaks of 'entreaties', 'prayers', 'petitions' and 'thanksgivings'. Prayer also has many depths that we can plumb. For instance, Daniel's prayers initiate angelic conflict in heaven; Peter's prayers have an intensity that causes him to fall into a trance (Acts 10;10); and Paul's prayers, like that of John's, result in him being caught up into heaven! (II Corinthians 12:2)

> **However, like many other areas of our Christian life, prayer is a growing matter and we shall only get to its 'depths' if we begin at the surface.**

Those who turn the soil at the surface will ultimately reach the 'riches' of the depths. In other words, all God wants is men and women who will enroll in the school of prayer. He will take care of the education and the ability as long as we are willing! God is wanting countless thousands to graduate as 'watchmen'. The question is – when will we respond to His call?

Watchmen

In this end time, watchmen are urgently required in order to guard the gates of the nations and particularly the gates of Israel. A gate is an entry or exit point – to state the obvious. However, for too long the spiritual gates of the nations have been left 'watchmenless' – or, unguarded.

The enemy has therefore marched in unhindered and has ravaged and bespoiled the nations. The serious biblical scholar is aware of the fact that physical realities are really the visible manifestations of unseen, but very real, spiritual realities.

For instance, Scripture reveals that men and women reject God's love in Jesus because an unseen demonic power has blinded their eyes:

> 'And even if our gospel is veiled, it is veiled to those who are perishing, in whose case the God of this world has blinded the minds of the unbelieving that they might not see the light of the gospel of the glory of Christ, who is the image of God.'   (II Corinthians 4:3–4 NASB)

Now, not until this demonic power is dealt with, will men and women be free to accept Christ Jesus the Saviour. Whole nations and groups of nations – i.e. the communist bloc – are in visible chaos and wickedness because of demonic rulers and forces that are controlling and manipulating them in the invisible sphere (Daniel 11, Revelation 12). For this reason Paul said that 'Our struggle is not against flesh and blood, but against the rulers, against the powers, against the world forces of this darkness, against the spiritual forces of wickedness in heavenly places.' (Ephesians 6:12)

Our nations are in turmoil, anguish and chaos because the watchmen of the Lord have abandoned their watch.

Watchmen are urgently required.

For too long we have dismissed the vital and important place that watchful prayer occupies in the economy and purposes of God.

When will we change this situation? A watchman is a warrior and a protector. He knows how to defend his city against the enemy and he also knows how to go out and neutralise the enemy before he attacks. In other words, as spiritual watchmen we are not only to defend that which is ours, but, we are to enlarge our borders by taking territory held by the devil. We are to assault the 'gates of hell' and rescue those held captive behind them! (Matthew 16:18) Indeed Paul says that the weapons of our warfare are of divine origin and thus capable of tearing down the enemies' strongholds and fortresses (II Corinthians 10:4–5). When will we begin to use them?

It is through watchful prayer that we prepare any people or nation or church for the acts of God.

However, as Jerusalem is the 'gate' through which the Kingdom of God, in its visible and physical form, will be ushered into our world, it is essential that watchmen should begin to arise who will determine from henceforth who will enter her gates. The time has come to claim Jerusalem for the 'King of Kings' and only as watchmen, from all over the world, gather to her walls for defence and attack, will the way be prepared for Him to return and take His rightful throne. Isaiah put it this way:

'On your walls, O Jerusalem, I have appointed watchmen; All day and all night they will never keep silent. You who remind the Lord take no rest for yourselves; And give Him no rest until He establishes and makes Jerusalem a praise in the earth.'
(Isaiah 62:6–7 NASB)

The 'watchman' or 'gatekeeper's' ministry is therefore one in which every child of God must be involved. It is not reserved for any 'class' of Christian. No, it embraces all of God's people and it involves simple prayer. That is, prayer that is sincere, fired by the Word of God and that comes from the heart. That is why every Christian should be praying. When will it happen?

They were placed in a position of trust

'All these who were chosen to be gatekeepers in the thresholds were 212. These were enrolled by genealogy in their villages, whom David and Samuel the seer appointed in their office of trust.'

(I Chronicles 9:22 NASB)

In other words, the security and well-being of God's house and kingdom on earth were in their hands. The gatekeepers took up their positions on the 'thresholds'. A threshold constitutes the dividing line between two entities. It is an entry point. In the work of God it is a line of demarcation between the kingdom of light and the kingdom of darkness (Colossians 1:13–14).

The gatekeepers were therefore required to keep the enemy at bay. They were 'guards':

'So they and their sons had charge of the gates of the house of the Lord, even the house of the tent, as guards.'

(I Chronicles 9:23 NASB)

We, too, are to occupy the 'thresholds' and by so doing keep the devil and his demons from ravaging the kingdom of God. This is a position of trust, that is, the well-being of our nations and churches depends on the 'gatekeepers' or 'watchmen'.

> **It is essential for us to note that Jesus cannot return to Jerusalem and, thus to the earth, unless the watchmen first take their place and prepare the way for him through prayer.**

As we respond to this call, not only will the day of redemption dawn in Israel but the whole world will be brought nearer to the day of Messiah's reign.

Watchmen enjoy the privilege of giving 'right of entry'. Their discretion is authoritative and final. A constant band of watchmen, standing at the gates of Israel and praying in the light of God's Word and revealed will, can, and will in the end, usher in the coming of Jesus. This is so because, as time passes, their authority can grow to a point where only the King can enter Jerusalem and therefore must come again. In this respect it is important for us to note Isaiah 62:1–2:

> 'For Zion's sake I will not keep silent, and for Jerusalem's sake I will not keep quiet, until her righteousness goes forth like brightness, and her salvation like a torch that is burning. And the nations will see your righteousness, and all kings your glory . . .'

The need is for watchmen, and I have no doubt that God the Holy Spirit is seeking to call them forth today. This is the day when He is fulfilling His promise to appoint watchmen on the walls of Jerusalem. By the use of spiritual weapons they will withstand the devil and admit King Jesus into our world. This Holy work of prayer must be done 'For The World's Sake!'

So then watchmen are required in order for God to birth and bring forth His final triumph in the world.

When will we as believers, finally recognise this?

Praying with heart, understanding and commitment

These watchmen will, in the first place, seek to be close to the heart of God in order that they may fully understand the times in which they are living and, as a result, pray in harmony with His purposes. They will thus be like the sons of Issachar, 'men who understand the times, with knowledge of what Israel should do . . .' (I Chronicles 12:32) Or, they

100

will be like Jesus who, in the days of His earthly pilgrimage, did nothing of Himself but only that which he saw His Father doing (John 5:19). The watchmen appointed by God follow in this tradition. In short, they know their God and therefore rise up to do exploits in His name! (Daniel 11:32)

Secondly, they are men and women of commitment. That is, they stay at their post no matter what!

In I Chronicles chapter nine we are given a wonderful picture of the responsibilities and required commitment of watchmen or gatekeepers. It is important for us to note the following:

They were taken from the sons of Levi – that is, they came from the priestly tribe

> 'Now the gatekeepers were Shallum and Akkub and Talmon and Ahiman and their relatives (Shallum the chief being stationed until now at the king's gate to the east). These were the gatekeepers for the camp of the sons of Levi.' (I Chronicles 9:17–18 NASB)

The New Testament declares that all blood-washed believers have become a part of God's priesthood.

> 'To Him who loves us, and released us from our sins by His blood, and He has made us to be a kingdom, priests to His God and Father, to Him be the glory and dominion forever and ever. Amen.' (Revelation 1:5–6 NASB)

It is important for us to also note that our position of trust is chiefly exercised and discharged before God. We are accountable to God for the condition of His work on earth! When will we realise this?

Samuel well recognised this and therefore affirmed that he would not sin before God by ceasing to pray for Israel and for Saul, her first king.

> 'Moreover, as for me, far be it from me that I should sin against the Lord by ceasing to pray for you ...' (I Samuel 12:23 NASB)

We have sinned as we have abandoned the 'thresholds'.

As we examine the state of our churches and of our world we can only conclude that we have sinned as we have abandoned the 'thresholds' and have allowed the enemy to infiltrate, disrupt, corrupt and destroy. When will we change this?

The time has surely come for all of us to arise and reassume our prayer positions at the threshold of our churches, our nations and of Israel. It must be remembered that God presently rules the world through, or, by means of, the prayers of His people on earth (Psalm 149:5–9). As they assume this responsibility, honour and position of trust, the benefits of Jesus' death are appropriated on behalf of the world (Ephesians 1:9–10).

Ultimately the very physical world will become His (Revelation 11:15). But ... all this will only happen when God's children begin to pray. By so doing, the most humble, insignificant saint can initiate conflict in the heavenlies that will eventually have visible redemptive outworkings on the earth!

> **Prayer discharged as a trust before God causes us to be co-workers with Him as He unfolds His redemptive plan for the world.** **(II Corinthians 6:1–2)**

When will we embrace this privilege?

They were to keep a special watch facing the east

> 'Now the gatekeepers were Shallum and Akkub and Talmon and Ahiman and their relatives (Shallum the chief being stationed until now at the king's gate to the east). (I Chronicles 9:17–18)

In Scripture 'the east' always speaks of the coming of God into our world. For instance the temple faced eastward (Ezekiel 43:1, 47:1) and its doors, when opened, according to the prophet Ezekiel, permitted the first rays of sunlight to shine in as the sun topped the Mount of Olives, which, as we all know, is to the east of Jerusalem (Ezekiel 8:16).

Naturally, this was a symbol of God's glory entering the temple:

> 'Then he led me to the gate, the gate facing toward the east; and behold, the glory of the God of Israel was coming from the way of the east. And His voice was like the sound of many waters; and the earth shone with His glory.' (Ezekiel 43:1–2)

The watchmen, looking toward the east, are therefore looking and praying for the coming of the King of glory. This is our responsibility as praying watchmen. Jesus said that as the lightning comes from the east and flashes to the west, so shall the day of His coming be (Matthew 24:27).

The only road upon which Jesus can travel as He comes from heaven to earth, a second time, is the road of prayer. This is the day for us to arise and begin building a highway for our God! This is part of our commitment. When will we shoulder it?

Israel needs her king and so does the world and we as His believing people need to constantly pray, 'Amen. Come, Lord Jesus' (Revelation 22:20).

They faced all directions and covered every entry and exit point

> 'The gatekeepers were on the four sides, to the east, west, north and south.'   (I Chronicles 9:24 NASB)

In other words, every part of God's work was protected. There were no gaps anywhere.

> **The 'watchmen ministry' is to undergird every activity undertaken in the name of Jesus.**

When will we learn this? Many of the difficulties presently besetting the church of God are not because of a lack of activity, professionalism or expertise among the ministers or clergy. No, the 'house of the Lord' very often suffers from one spiritual disease or another because we have given little priority to prayer. We have concentrated on 'methods' and 'principles' as if a special formula is all that is required, and we have ignored prayer! In short we have sought solutions in every sphere other than prayer – **the right one**.

Ministers and local church leaders suggest from one conference to another learning about church growth, time

The real need is prayer!

management, leadership skills and worship technics – all to no avail. The real need is prayer ... prayer for our churches, our cities, our nations and for Israel, the key to world redemption! Yes, this is the day to station watchmen or gatekeepers on all four sides, 'to the east, west, north and south.'

They protected the chambers and treasuries in the house of God

'For the four chief gatekeepers who were Levites, were in an office of trust, and were over the chambers and over the treasuries in the house of God.' (I Chronicles 9:26)

The above Scripture teaches that the precious things in the house of God were placed in the care of the gatekeepers. The enemy always seeks to destroy these things so that the house of God can be kept barren, poverty stricken and of no use to God in the world. When will we grasp this?

> **Much precious truth has been stolen from the church because we have neglected to station prayer watchmen over her.**

The result has been 'doctrines of men' couched very often in intellectualism and cleverness of the natural mind. Not least of these has been the 'replacement theory' that has transferred all the blessings and good promises that God made to Israel, to the church. Conveniently the curses still apply to Israel!

This 'theory', which has taken root in many Christian circles, leaves Israel with no future and her modern day restoration is considered as being nothing more than a political accident! It is a lie from hell and its 'fruit' has been wicked and destructive, to say the least. Much of the anti-Semitism of our world owes its origins to the 'replacement theory' – and, this is also true of the Nazi Holocaust in which six million Jews died, one-and-a-half million being children!

How did this terrible thing happen? I believe it happened through prayerlessness, which allowed the devil to come in and rob the church of the precious truth concerning Israel.

A casual glance at the book of Acts reveals that the early church was saturated with prayer and, as a result, with truth. Many indeed are the references to her frequent prayer meetings. The 'gatekeepers' were firmly placed over the precious things in the house of God. As a result, there was an explosion of truth.

However, as the first century came to an end, the concentration and emphasis changed and so more attention was given to doctrinal discussion than to prayer. The result: the devil stripped the church, as one peels an onion, of all vital truth. Eventually, by the time of the middle ages, the church was totally 'bankrupt', poverty stricken and of no use to God in the world. Even the most important and most precious truth of all – namely, justification by faith – was gone! How did all this happen? Because the prayer watchmen had abandoned their watch!

It is interesting to note that the more churchmen discussed

truth during this dark period, so the more they lost it! On the other hand the gradual process of restoration that began in the fifteenth century had its beginnings with earnest, soul-searching prayer. Martin Luther was a man of prayer. He spent a minimum of two hours a day in prayer – no wonder the fire of God filled his soul and gave birth to truth. At last a real watchman had been raised up and as a result the precious things began to return to the house of God. Every revival from Luther's day onwards has been punctuated by prayer and the restoration of truth. A casual glance at church history will confirm and underline this. When will we recognise the relationship between prayer and truth?

> **Prayer 'washes' the mind so that it can better understand the truth of God's Word.**

For me, it is very significant that the men presently responsible under God for restoring 'Israel truth' to the church are all men of prayer and part of the 'World Intercessors' movement. In this connection, we need simply mention Lance Lambert, Derek Prince, Johannes Facius and Kjell Sjoberg. All these men have made a major contribution to the work of God in the world and are greatly respected.

The fact that at this time God is speaking to the church about the important place that Israel occupies in His plan of world redemption means that the coming of the King and the birth of His visible kingdom of peace is now nigh. As we enter this final stage of present world history, may we all take our place as 'gatekeepers' guarding the precious truths that have been, and are being, deposited in the house of God!

Their watch was continuous and without end

'And they spent the night around the house of God, because the watch was committed to them; and they were in charge of opening it morning by morning.'

(I Chronicles 9:27)

The first century church witnessed the birthing of the kingdom of God coming as it did with power. This birthing was only made possible because of men and women who had discovered the art of praying day and night!

> 'I thank God, whom I serve with a clear conscience the way my forefathers did, as I constantly remember you in my prayers night and day ...'
>
> (II Timothy 1:3 NASB)

This in no way means that Paul did nothing else but pray. We all know this from his life story and in I Thessalonians 2:9 he also makes mention of the fact that he worked night and day. So, what did he really mean when he wrote about praying night and day? He was referring to a lifestyle. In other words, in the midst of life's many activities, prayer became as natural to him as is the constant inhaling of fresh air.

Another way of putting it is to say that Paul's life was a prayer to God. He lived in constant communion with His God and Saviour and was thus unceasing in prayer (I Thessalonians 5:17). No wonder so much of God's purposes for the world in his day were birthed through him!

Our century is about to witness the birthing of the kingdom of God, coming as it will with 'signs to be observed'. More than ever before the urgent need is for 'spiritual campers', that is, men and women who will persevere in prayer – night and day.

Prayer that really moves God is prayer that gives Him no rest!

When will we rise to meet this challenge? Scripture affirms that a 'time' is coming – one filled with gross darkness, when no man will be able any longer to work the works of God (John 9:4). As we still have a little time left to us, let us resolve to use it by becoming 'gatekeepers' or 'watchmen' of the Lord.

For Israel and THE WORLD'S SAKE such a commitment is urgently required!

108

Prayer is our constant battle cry.

Chapter 9

How?

'And when you pray, you are not to be as the hypocrites ...'
(Matthew 6:5 NASB)

Prayer cannot really be taught; it is developed through experience. There are, however, a number of vital principles that govern it. When the disciples asked Jesus to teach them how to pray, He responded by outlining the basic principles of prayer.

In fact, He never gave them much teaching at all about the subject but He did teach them by frequent example. Indeed it was their seeing Him in regular prayer that prompted their enquiry about the subject in the first place (Luke 11:1–4).

The same is true of Paul. His epistles are full of exhortations to the believers to pray but in none of them does he give any extensive teaching about the 'hows' of prayer.

Prayer is like worship. It cannot be taught but it must be 'caught'.

It is probably true to say that much of our teaching about prayer really comes from the true life accounts of some of the great men of God in Scripture. In this connection we need simply think of Abraham, Samuel, David, Elijah, Job, Paul

111

and many others. Their prayer 'lifestyles' become our real tutor about the subject, and the abiding lesson for all of us is this: each one of us has to develop our own lifestyle of prayer. This, of course, is a never-ending process.

> **The method of prayer is unimportant. What really matters is having a real relationship with God.**

History affirms that men have resorted to all sorts of methods – some of them most bizarre – in order to establish regular, intelligent and meaningful communion with the Saviour. The 'closet' of Scripture (Matthew 6:6) can be a room, a desert, a train, a church building, a forest, a beach or an aeroplane. The lesson for all of us is clear: go anywhere where you can be alone with God!

So, prayer begins with taking concrete steps to be alone with God. For this reason Scripture recommends the early morning for those who wish to take their relationship with God seriously.

> 'Since the day that your fathers came out of the land of Egypt, until this day, I have sent you all My servants the prophets, daily rising early and sending them.'
> (Jeremiah 7:25 NASB)

> 'And in the early morning, while it was still dark, He arose and went out and departed to a lonely place, and was praying there.' (Mark 1:35 NASB)

The early morning provides us with quietness and frees us from the hustle and bustle of each day's activities. It is, however, important to note that nowhere does Scripture command prayer in the early morning. The burden of Scripture is that God's people should give themselves to regular prayer at a time when they can give God their undivided attention.

The early morning happens to the best time for most of us, but, if you can give God your undivided attention at some

The 'closet' of Scripture can be ... anywhere where you can be alone with God!

other time of the day, well and good. The all important thing is that we spend a good portion of each day in conversation with God.

> **God wants your fellowship. Prayer brings reality into your spiritual life.**

The principles of prayer

Jesus outlined the principles of prayer in His famous teaching now known everywhere as 'The Lord's Prayer.'

'And He said to them, "When you pray, say: Father, hallowed be Thy name, Thy kingdom come, Give us each day our daily bread, and forgive us our sins, for we ourselves also forgive everyone who is indebted to us. And lead us not into temptation."' (Luke 11:2–4 NASB)

We should take note of the following:

Prayer should be an act of worship

'Father, hallowed be Thy name ...' (Luke 11:2 NASB)

Man was created to worship God (Ecclesiastes 12:13). The recreation of man 'in Christ' provides him with an opportunity to express his reason for living. Paul describes this truth by saying that we who are the redeemed of God should 'be to the praise of His glory' (Ephesians 1:12).

Men and women who worship God regularly experience real inner health – their lives are characterised by a contentment that comes from within and which is not dependent upon external circumstances. Christians lose this inner health and contentment when they neglect prayer and worship. Any relationship with God should be firmly based upon a recognition of His great love, mercy and goodness and of our perpetual unworthiness. This gives God His rightful place in our lives and it keeps us happy!

> **Worship is nothing more than man finding his rightful place in God's creation.**

Prayer should be an expression of our desire to fit in with the concerns of God's Kingdom

'Thy Kingdom come,
Thy will be done,
On earth as it is in heaven ...' (Matthew 6:10 NASB)

Fellowship with God means doing things with Him! Paul writes to the Corinthian believers and states that we are called to be co-workers with God in the world.

114

'And working together with Him, we also urge you not
to receive the grace of God in vain ...'

(II Corinthians 6:1)

God's love for and appreciation of us is such that He does
not want us to work for Him but with Him. Together with
God we work out His redemptive plans for the world. This,
quite obviously, is an exciting privilege. However, only regular prayer will keep us close to His heart so that we can work
in harmony with His will and know or understand the times
and seasons in which we are living.

It is important for us to know that some things cannot be
taught by dogma, but only by regular contact with God
through prayer! An understanding of the days in which we
are living is a case in question, as is an appreciation of the
love of God. In this connection, note I Thessalonians 4:9.

'Now as to the love of the brethren, you have no need for
anyone to write to you, for you yourselves are taught by
God to love one another ...'

and

'Now as to the times and the epochs, brethren, you have
no need of anything to be written you ...'

(I Thessalonians 5:1)

In these two verses Paul takes it for granted that Christians are close enough to God so as to understand His purposes. In this context, how many in the church, because of
prayer, have discerned and understood the intentions of God
concerning Israel?

Dogma and rigid eschatological theories have all too often
been given precedence over prayer. We frequently hear of
this conference and that conference – all dealing with doctrinal subjects, and commendably so – but, rarely, if ever, do
we hear of a prayer conference!

In many believing circles therefore, a 'body' has been
fashioned that cannot readily respond to the wishes and
promptings of the 'Head'. Christ's body is paralysed and

Most of the men of God presently involved in the world intercessors movement also have a real understanding and insight into the purposes of God for Israel.

cannot work with Him in the world ... as it doesn't understand 'The times and epochs'.

It is certainly no coincidence that most of the men of God presently involved in the world intercessors movement also have a real understanding and insight into the purposes of God for Israel. In all of their lives, prayer is the common denominator. In John 12:26, Jesus refers to the prayerful Christian in the following terms:

> 'If anyone serves Me, let him follow Me; and where I am, there shall My servant be; if anyone serves Me, the Father will honour him ...'

To follow Christ as he accomplishes His will in the earth means that we need to be close to His heart. Only regular

116

prayer makes this possible. It is important for us to note that Jesus is always 'changing locations'. He describes His constant movement by saying, '... and where I am' ...; meaning that the concentration of Divine attention changes from time to time. Only those in tune with His heart will be able to discern a 'concentration change' and act accordingly. Jesus says, '... Where I am there My servant will be also ...'

We need to ask ourselves, 'Where is Jesus today?' What issues are presently the focus of His attention? 'For The World's Sake' we need to know these things! Christians who can answer these questions are honoured. Maybe because they are so few in number!

Prayer is the place where our daily living needs are to be expressed

'Give us each day our daily bread ...'

(Luke 11:3 NASB)

'Bread' in this passage is a symbol of our daily living requirements. God wants us to ask Him about these things as He longs to reveal His Fatherhood love and faithfulness to us.

> **The needs of life, if brought before God in prayer, will teach us more about His character and faithfulness than anything else.**

This indeed was the thrust of Jesus's sermon on the mount. In spite of this many of us still have much difficulty in believing that our Father in heaven can take care of the most trivial concern. The truth is, He can and wants to! We need to be reminded that Jesus said:

'Do not be anxious then, saying, 'What shall we eat?' or 'What shall we drink' or 'With what shall we clothe ourselves?'

For all these things the Gentiles eagerly seek; for your Heavenly Father knows that you need all these things ...'

(Matthew 6:31–32 NASB)

117

It is important for us to note that our Father in heaven looks after our *daily needs* (Matthew 6:34). Human nature would dearly love Him to take care of our monthly, if not our yearly needs. However, if He did this we would never learn anything about His character.

Looking to Him, through prayer, on a daily basis for the basic provisions of life is an exciting on-going way of discovering what He is like.

> **Christians who trust God for much, also know much about His character.**

Prayer should be an expression of our desire to be right with God and with our fellow man

'... forgive us our sins, for we ourselves also forgive everyone who is indebted to us.'   (Luke 11:4 NASB)

Men and women who pray regularly have the touch of God upon their lives and enjoy healthy relationships with their fellow men.

> **A prayerless Christian is a walking prickly pear!**

In many ways, prayer is a healthy and important safeguard against broken relationships. People who pray regularly find it well nigh impossible to be in a relationship breakdown with others. The reason is simple. If such a breakdown did exist, then they would not be able to pray regularly! Heaven will be like brass; no reply would come from the 'throne' and the reality of God's presence would be gone. God expects us to forgive others as He forgives us.

'For if you forgive men for their transgressions, your heavenly Father will also forgive you. But if you do not forgive men, then your Father will not forgive your transgressions.' (Matthew 6:14–15 NASB)

Indeed, it is important to underline the fact that if we do not forgive others their sins against us, then God will not forgive us our sins.

> **Unforgiveness shuts us out from God's redemptive love.**

If unforgiveness persists we shall find ourselves ravaged by the demonic forces of the enemy. Jesus said that one who stubbornly harbours unforgiveness against another will, in the end, be handed over to 'the torturer!'

'Then summoning him, his lord said to him, "You wicked slave, I forgave you all that debt because you entreated me. Should you not also have had mercy on your fellow slave, even as I had mercy on you?"
And his lord, moved with anger, handed him over to the torturers until he should pay all that was owed him ...' (Matthew 18:32–34 NASB)

Paul writing to the Corinthians recognised the same truth. In the light of it he exhorted the believers to forgive an offending brother for; if they did not, they would provide the enemy with an opportunity to come in and cause havoc among the believing community.

'Sufficient for such a one is this punishment which was inflicted by the majority, so that on the contrary *you should rather forgive and comfort him*, lest somehow such a one be overwhelmed by excessive sorrow. Wherefore I urge you to reaffirm your love for him. For to this end also I wrote that I might put you to the test, whether you are obedient in all things. But whom you forgive anything, I forgive also; for indeed what I have forgiven, if I have forgiven anything, I did it for your sakes in the

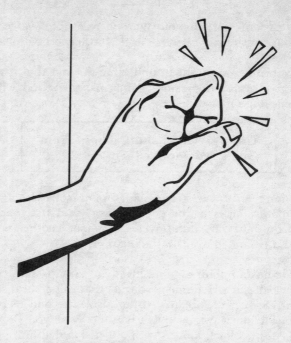

Jesus is always knocking on our heart's door.

presence of Christ, *in order that no advantage be taken of us by Satan; for we are not ignorant of his schemes.'*

(II Corinthians 2:6–11 NASB)

The story of Judas Iscariot is no doubt recorded in Scripture as a warning to all of us. His on-going problem with money (John 12:4–6) led him to a place where he harboured a grudge against Jesus (Mark 14:10). Moreover, his persistent refusal to rectify this situation, in spite of Jesus' attempts to bring him to repentance and forgiveness (John 13:26), eventually brought him to the tragic place where, Scripture declares, 'Satan entered into him' (John 13:27). Cut off from the redemptive love of God he found himself tortured by the devil and in the end destroyed! (Acts 1:17–20)

Yes, many believing communities throughout the world are presently being ravaged by the devil because we, the children of God, have given him much opportunity by our unforgiving hearts! By contrast, Scripture says,

> 'Be angry, and yet do not sin; do not let the sun go down on your anger, and do not give the devil an opportunity.'
> (Ephesians 4:26–27 NASB)

It must be noted from the 'Lord's Prayer' that the request that we should not be led into the evil of temptation is in the context of repentance and our willingness to forgive others (Luke 11:4).

> **To gain the ear of God we must be right with Him and with our fellow man.**

NOTE: Being right with our fellow man means doing everything possible from our side to rectify the situation. Paul puts it this way:

> 'Pursue peace with all men ...' (Hebrews 12:14 NASB)

> *and*

> 'See that no one repays another with evil for evil, but always seek after that which is good for one another and for all men.'   (I Thessalonians 5:15 NASB)

> *and*

> 'Never pay back evil for evil to anyone. Respect what is right in the sight of all men. If possible, so far as it depends on you, be at peace with all men.'
> (Romans 12:17–18 NASB)

The great need in the church is for men and women who enjoy the ear of God. Such people can and will change the world. 'For The World's Sake' and for Israel's good let us be a people characterised by forgiveness!

Perhaps the most important principle of prayer is: *Get started!*

People who begin to pray, bearing in mind the four basic principles above, will discover, as time passes, that their experience of prayer will deepen and vary, including their methods, until they settle into a lifestyle of prayer that best serves their communion with God.

Moreover, as they become regular and consistent in prayer, the Holy Spirit can begin to shape their prayers and use them in ways that best serve the interests of God's kingdom here on earth. So, in time, their prayers will become thanksgivings, entreaties, supplications and intercessions.

> **What prayer becomes is the Holy Spirit's concern! Our concern is to merely appreciate the importance of prayer and give ourselves to it regularly.**

In many ways, prayer is like flying a kite. Once in the air the wind does with the kite as it wills. One minute blowing it in this direction and then in the other. Sometimes the kite dives toward the ground and at other times it soars straight up toward the clouds. The wind constantly dictates the path and nature of the kite's flight.

As we regularly launch the kite of prayer into the wind of the Holy Spirit, He will determine, by His will alone, the nature of our prayers. One day we may find ourselves overcome with thanksgiving and praise and then on another we may find ourselves in deep anguish of spirit about a certain matter.

> **The true nature of prayer is determined by our regular commitment to it.**

The most successful pray-ers of history have been those who made prayer a regular daily feature of their lives. This

In many ways, prayer is like flying a kite.

and this alone was the key to their power with God. Take Daniel for instance. Of him Scripture says, 'And he continued kneeling on his knees three times a day, praying and giving thanks before his God, as he had been doing previously.'

Neither was David a stranger to regular prayer, for in Psalm 55:17 he declares, 'Evening and morning and at noon, I will complain and murmur and He will hear my voice.'

Jesus also developed the habit of regular prayer and Luke 5:16 says, 'He Himself would often slip away to the wilderness and pray.'

By regular prayer the Holy Spirit will birth through us, intercessions, thanksgivings and entreaties. Note I Timothy 2:1.

> 'First of all, then, I urge that entreaties and prayers, petitions and thanksgivings be made on behalf of all men.'

123

Intercessions

Intercessions, referred to as petitions in the above translation, are a form of prayer that causes us, not simply to pray about people, but, to long so much for their salvation, blessing and good that we are willing to assume their place in life before God. It is the prayer of desired self-destruction!

> 'I am telling the truth in Christ, I am not lying, my conscience bearing me witness in the Holy Spirit, that I have great sorrow and unceasing grief in my heart. For I could wish that I myself were accursed, separated from Christ for the sake of my brethren, my kinsmen according to the flesh . . .'   (Romans 9:1–3 NASB)

Moses, contemplating the wickedness and failure of his brethren, petitioned God in the same way.

> 'And it came about on the next day that Moses said to the people, "You yourselves have committed a great sin; and now I am going up to the Lord, perhaps I can make atonement for your sin."
> Then Moses returned to the Lord, and said, "Alas, this people has committed a great sin, and they have made a god of gold for themselves. But now, if Thou wilt, forgive their sin – and if not, please blot me out from Thy book which Thou hast written!"'
> (Exodus 32:30–32 NASB)

This type of prayer can save whole nations and has! It saved Israel in Moses' day. However, it is important to note that examples of it in Scripture and in history are infrequent. Much of what goes under the name of intercession today is nothing more than dedicated prayer requests. It is important for us to know this so that we are not overawed and thus deterred from praying ourselves when we hear so many folk claiming for themselves and speaking glibly of the ministry of intercession. If God wants you in intercession He will do it! Your responsibility is simply to 'fly your kite'. Above all let us pray that God will raise up real intercessors for Israel 'For The World's Sake'.

Thanksgiving

This form of prayer is initiated by God's goodness to us. It is our prayerful response to the self revelation of God. As God reveals His love, power, faithfulness and care to us, we respond appropriately by the giving of thanks to His name.

Thanksgiving should be a regular feature of our prayer lives as we can never cease giving thanks for the great salvation that God has provided for us in His Son Jesus.

For this reason Scripture exhorts us to come before His presence with thanksgiving. All of life's experiences are to be faced with thanksgiving.

> 'In everything give thanks: for this is God's will for you in Christ Jesus.' (I Thessalonians 5:18 NASB)

God is greater than our trials and difficulties and therefore even in adverse circumstances we can and must still look to Him with thanksgiving in our hearts.

Let us in particular give thanks for the restoration of Israel as we continue to call upon God to complete this precious work.

Entreaties

These constitute the daily and urgent requests of God's children. This is the most common form of prayer and God delights to answer it – in His way!

God always answers prayer, sometimes by not giving us what we desire.

> **Silence is sometimes God's most appropriate answer to some of our misguided prayers.**

In all our entreaties we are to let God be God. Very often our real understanding of certain situations is so limited that if God did what we asked Him to do we would end up in a deep ditch.

On looking back over my life I can, with much thanksgiving, bless God for not answering at least 50 per cent of my prayers in the way I thought appropriate. If He had I would have been in serious difficulty by now – perhaps even dead!

Believers who fail to appreciate this mystery in prayer very often end up in discouragement and bewilderment. Jesus warned us against this in Luke 18:1:

> 'Now He was telling them a parable to show that at all times they ought to pray and not lose heart.'

Notice that prayer requests are to be made to God 'at all times'. God is interested in every detail of our lives, even the small insignificant ones. No action or activity under the sun is exempt from His concern and scrutiny.

Naturally, that which concerns Him most is His redemptive plan, in Jesus, for the world. Israel and the church are at the very heart of this plan and should feature regularly in our entreaties.

Israel is at the very heart of God's redemptive plan, in Jesus, for the world.

Chapter 10

What?

'O Lord God of hosts,
How long wilt Thou be angry with the prayer of Thy people?
    Thou hast fed them with the bread of tears,
And Thou hast made them to drink tears in large measure.
Thou dost make us an object of contention to our neighbours;
    And our enemies laugh among themselves.
        O God of hosts, restore us,
And cause Thy face to shine upon us, and we will be saved.
                            (Psalm 80:4–7 NASB)

Israel's prayer requirements

No consideration of Israel's prayer requirements would be complete without some reference to the urgent needs that face the country. Our prayers on behalf of Israel are to be intelligent and specific. In order to pray in this way we need to acquaint ourselves more fully with the facts.

The book of Nehemiah, dealing as it does with Israel's restoration 70 years after her deportation to Babylon in 586 BC, has much to teach us concerning Israel's present day restoration after nearly 2000 years of exile.

In chapter three of the book, specific gates are repaired in the process of restoration, and these gates remind us of the work that has yet to be completed in Israel's modern day restoration.

Gates and prayer needs

Each gate then represents a particular prayer need and, since God has called us to be gatekeepers of the nation in a spiritual sense, by examining these gates we will be better equipped to faithfully discharge our priestly ministry in this regard.

We would, of course, do well to remember that God delights to answer specific prayer – even though it is always far easier to pray in general and vague terms such as, 'Lord bless Israel'.

However, while some form of prayer on behalf of Israel is better than no prayer, it is still true that prayer couched in vague and very general terms will accomplish precious little.

God is looking for committed 'watchmen' or 'gatekeepers' who will believe Him for 'specifics' and in so doing give real impetus to the pace of restoration. As always this type of 'prayer watchman' is not easily found as the demands are great and the immediate rewards are so few – and yet, those who rise to this challenge will in the end be a vital part of God's redemptive plan for the world. Paul knew something of this high calling and privilege as he considered that his life was, in some strange way, contributing to Christ's redemptive sufferings on behalf of the world.

> 'Now I rejoice in my sufferings for your sake, and in my flesh I do my share on behalf of His Body (which is the church) in filling up that which is lacking in Christ's afflictions.'   (Colossians 1:24 NASB)

Paul was therefore a partner or co-worker with God in His vineyard, the earth (II Corinthians 6:1). God is still looking for partners or co-workers as they are desperately needed 'For The World's Sake!'

A closer look at Nehemiah chapter three reveals that we are to assume our prayer watch at the following gates:

1. The Sheep Gate

> 'Then Eliashib the high priest arose with his brothers
> the priests and built the Sheep Gate; they consecrated it
> and hung its doors ...'   (Nehemiah 3:1 NASB)

We should be in constant prayer for the regathering of the
exiles to the land of Israel.

There are approximately 15 million Jews in the world. To
date only four million have returned from the four corners of
the earth to their ancient and God given homeland, Israel.

In real terms, this means that not even one-third of world
Jewry lives in Israel. The 'Sheep' are still scattered upon
every mountain top and only specific prayer in this regard
will bring them home to their proper sheepfold. Quite
obviously the comforts of a Western style of living – in most
cases – has much to do with their refusal to come home and
we need to pray that they will somehow be shaken loose from
their attachment to things.

The question of the approximately two million Jews in
Russia is a different matter, since they are virtually held
captive by the Soviet regime. However, many of them, when
given liberty to leave do not return to Israel but usually end
up in America. This is something of an embarrassment to
Israel and we need to pray that they will return to Israel
upon gaining official permission to leave Russia.

In the final analysis the nations of the world are no refuge
place for the Jewish community. History has proved this and
will continue to do so. The only safe place for world Jewry,
which also appears to be the most unlikely, is Israel. Dr
Theodore Herzl, the father, in many ways, of the modern state
of Israel came to this conclusion after considering the position
of world Jewry in the 'Diaspora' – and, Jabotinsky, one of the
early Zionist leaders, called upon European Jewry to go home
to Israel. This he did before the outbreak of the Second World
War! If only the Jewish community in Europe had listened to
him, for then the Nazi Holocaust would never have trans-
pired! In fact, Jabotinsky's warning still rings with urgency
today. He said, 'Unless European Jewry liquidate themselves
from the Diaspora the Diaspora will liquidate them!'

Somehow it is almost as if some step of faith is required from the Jewish community in order to return to Israel. Let us pray that God will give this gift of faith to them so that they will return to the land of their forefathers and in so doing, be able to look beyond the sacrifices that have to be made in this regard.

In short, let us rise up and repair the 'Sheep Gate'.

2. The Fish Gate

> 'Now the sons of Hassenaah built the Fish Gate; they laid its beams and hung its doors with its bolts and bars.'
> (Nehemiah 3:3 NASB)

Throughout Scripture Israel's physical restoration to the land always precedes her spiritual restoration to the Lord. In this respect it is important for us to note Ezekiel 36:23–25

> 'For I will take you from the nations, gather you from all the lands, and bring you into your own land.
> Then I will sprinkle clean water on you, and you will be clean; I will cleanse you from all your idols.'

The fact that God has restored the nation to the land means that their spiritual restoration is not too far off – and, with it the redemption of the world. Only believing prayer will remove the veil of unbelief presently covering the Jewish heart! I have no doubt that Jesus is beginning to fish for the Jewish heart. This will be a sovereign work of the Holy Spirit since the veil of unbelief was initially placed over the Jewish heart by a sovereign work of God.

> 'For I do not want you, brethren, to be uninformed of this mystery, lest you be wise in your own estimation, that a partial hardening has happened to Israel until the fullness of the Gentiles has come in; and thus all Israel will be saved; just as it is written,'
> 'The Deliverer will come from Zion,
> He will remove ungodliness from Jacob.'
> 'And this is My covenant with them,
> When I take away their sins.'
> (Romans 11:25–27 NASB)

God promises national redemption to no other nation except Israel. Among the nations He will gather in a remnant but of Israel the Word of God declares '... and thus all Israel will be saved.' This is a wonderful encouragement for those of us who have entered the prayer battle on her behalf. We have God's clear promise and Word to cling to. Let us rise up with the seed of God's Word in our hearts and let us repair the Fish Gate.

3. The Old Gate

'And Joiada the son of Paseah and Meshullam the son of Besodeiah repaired the Old Gate; they laid its beams and hung its doors, with its bolts and its bars.'

(Nehemiah 3:6 NASB)

The people of Israel need to discover the dynamic message proclaimed by their very own prophets of old. Unfortunately, their pathway to this discovery has been and is obscured in the main by religious legalism and extremism. Much of this religiosity has its roots in the external religious writings of the rabbinical sages. These writings have all too often complicated the simple and yet dynamic message of the Bible, leaving the man in the street bewildered and confused.

For many Israelis biblical religion is equated with a complicated system of rules, dogma and ritual. This causes them to shun the Bible and, in fact, in the country itself there is a deep division between the religious and secular communities. The secular community, which is by far the largest, is at present presented with little other religious alternative. For them the choice appears to be religious extremism or secularism. Being therefore unable to accept the heavy burdens of a religious life they have opted for secularism and humanism. Indeed, of late, a new brand of Judaism is emerging in an attempt to bridge the wide gap between the religious and secular communities. This brand of Judaism is called 'Secular Humanistic Judaism'. However, it is seriously flawed as it denies the existence of God and considers the Bible to be nothing more than a clever creation of man. So once again

Go through the gates.

the road back to the 'old way' is obscured by liberal thinking and the so-called cleverness of man.

The urgent need is for the man and woman in the street to embrace the refreshing and yet simple message of God's love contained in every book of the Bible. Only determined prayer will break through the mass of 'religious rubble' that presently obscures the way to the 'Old Gate'. Scripture exhorts us to pray in this way:

> 'Go through, go through the gates; clear the way for the people; build up, build up the highway; Remove the stones, lift up a standard over the peoples.
> Behold, the Lord has proclaimed to the end of the earth, say to the daughter of Zion, "Lo, your salvation comes" ...'   (Isaiah 62:10–11 NASB)

4. The Valley Gate

> 'Hanun and the inhabitants of Zanoah repaired the Valley Gate. They built it and hung its doors with its bolts and its bars ...'   (Nehemiah 3:13 NASB)

A valley speaks of separation. In our context it speaks of Israel rediscovering her trust in the God who formed her and created her for His glory. For too long Israel has put her trust in men, weapons and her own ingenuity.

However, the God of Abraham, Isaac and Jacob will have her as His own and therefore her difficulties will increase until there is no longer a human answer but only a Divine one! The God of heaven is steadily digging a valley around her and, in so doing, is slowly weaning her of every crutch that does not have a Divine origin. In a way we are witnessing the unfolding drama of an age-old love story. The God of history wants Israel to be exclusively His so that through her He may reveal His character to the nations. But she has turned in every direction except His and, in response, He is bringing more and more pressure to bear upon her so that in the end she will forsake all her earthly lovers and cling only to Him (Hosea 5:15).

We need to pray that, as Israel faces mounting difficulties at home and in the international arena, she will turn more and more to God and therefore separate herself from the instability and fickleness of trusting in men and in her own ability.

Above all, we need to pray that the ever increasing threat of war with her Arab neighbours will turn her gaze away from the United States of America and to the never-changing God of history.

Naturally, we do thank God for the protection and security that the U.S. has afforded and still does afford her. But, in the long run, this only causes Israel to misplace her trust and confidence. America's support of Israel is needed and we do pray that it may continue. At the same time, we need to pray that Israel will recognise the God who loves her and who ultimately is the only real guarantee of her security, protection and existence.

The time has come for us, through prayer, to build up the Valley Gate.

5. The Refuse Gate

'And Malchijah the son of Rechab, the official of the district of Bethhaccherem repaired the Refuse Gate ...'
(Nehemiah 3:14 NASB)

Like the other nations of our world, Israel also has much 'refuse' within her borders. By 'refuse' we mean the type of sin and iniquity that must ultimately attract and invite the judgment of God.

> 'For the wrath of God is revealed from heaven against all ungodliness and unrighteousness of men, who suppress the truth in unrighteousness.'
>
> (Romans 1:18 NASB)

From her very birth as a nation, Israel was called to be different from the other nations of the world and as such she was not to pollute herself with their sins and iniquities.

> 'When you enter the land which the Lord your God gives you, you shall not learn to imitate the detestable things of those nations.' (Deuteronomy 18:9 NASB)

It is interesting to note that while the founding fathers of the modern Jewish State were not religious, they nevertheless declared that they were seeking to found a nation that would be a 'light to the nations'.

Somehow the sense of their ancient and special calling has remained within them and even though they may still fail to acknowledge and serve the God of heaven as a nation, His initial charge to them is still resident in their hearts. We need to pray that this ancient calling will act as an umpire in their hearts, constantly warning them of the dangers of indulging in the sins of the nations.

In particular, Israel needs to be delivered from the social decadence that presently is so rampant in the Western world. There is no doubt in my mind that the Western world is fast becoming another Sodom and Gomorrah. Indeed, a close examinatin of the Scriptures reveals that the sin that most attracted the wrath of God in Lot's day was the sin of immorality and homosexuality (Genesis 19:4–11). The same is true of our day (Romans 1:18–32). In recent years, Western society has been permeated with this corruption to the very point of social acceptance and approval. So, in many nations

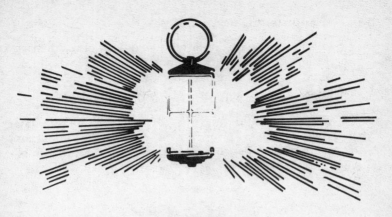

A light to the nations.

around the globe, homosexuals are defended, given special legal protection and even advanced to positions of authority in the church of the living God! This fact alone should warn us that the Day of Judgment is nigh. Indeed, Jesus said this very thing. As He gazed down the corridor of time to the day of His second coming, He said that that day would be preceded, and thus hastened, by forms of godlessness and rebellion which would demand the special judgment that could only be ushered in by His return.

> 'It was the same as happened in the days of Lot: they were eating, they were drinking, they were buying, they were selling, they were planting, they were building; but on the day that Lot went out from Sodom it rained fire and brimstone from heaven and destroyed them all. It will be just the same on the day that the Son of man is revealed.' (Luke 17:28–30 NASB)

In recent years, the decadence of Western society has begun to make alarming inroads in Israeli society. Abortion, immorality, homosexuality, drunkenness and ungodliness are all on the increase. The time has surely come for the 'Refuse Gate' to be repaired! Only fervent prayer will do it.

6. The Fountain Gate

> 'Shallum the son of Col-hozeh, the official of the district of Mizpah, repaired the Fountain Gate. He built it, covered it, and hung its doors with its bolts and its bars ...'
> (Nehemiah 3:15 NASB)

The whole of creation and the church, longs for the day when Israel will be a 'praise in the earth'. The 'Fountain Gate' speaks of a nation coming under the saturating rain of God's Spirit. Scripture promises that such a day will surely come.

> 'In that day a fountain will be opened for the house of David and for the inhabitants of Jerusalem, for sin and for impurity.'
> (Zechariah 13:1 NASB)

Naturally, this mighty outpouring of God's Spirit upon Israel will be closely linked to her redemption through Jesus, the Messiah. Again Zechariah states:

> 'And I will pour out on the house of David and on the inhabitants of Jerusalem, the Spirit of grace and of supplication, so that they will look on Me whom they have pierced; and they will mourn for Him, as one mourns for an only son ...'
> (Zechariah 12:10 NASB)

What a glorious day this will be! Israel's encounter with the Holy Spirit will unleash a sovereign work of God's Spirit throughout the earth. The nations will bask in God's glory and love and, so extensive will this work of the Spirit be that it can best be described as 'world drenching' or, as the prophet of old declared, it will be like the water covering the sea! That is, it will be extensive and embrace 'all flesh'.

Paul, contemplating this day, said that it would release an expression of God's power in the earth never seen before:

> 'For if their rejection be the reconciliation of the world, what will their acceptance be, but life from the dead?'
> (Romans 11:15 NASB)

However, it is important for us to realise that all this will not simply just happen! No, only believing prayer will usher it in. The 'rock' will only bring forth its water if it is struck with the rod of prayer!

The 'Fountain Gate' must be repaired. If we have any love for the nations, we will pray for the fountain in Israel to be restored. This is our urgent business 'For the World's Sake!'

7. The Water Gate

'And the temple servants living in Ophel made repairs as far as the front of the Water Gate toward the east and the projecting tower.'   (Nehemiah 3:26 NASB)

In the pages of Scripture, water is always a picture of the Word of God. For instance, Paul writes that believers are sanctified by the washing of the water of the Word of God (Ephesians 5:26).

There is no doubt that Israel needs to discover the power of her own Scriptures. This is more important than we think, as such a discovery will end the on-going controversy concerning who or what is a Jew? Indeed this controversy only continues to rage in Israel because, as a nation, she has largely discarded the Word of the Living God. This Word is mainly responsible for the Jewishness of Jews. As long as the Word of the Living God remains ignored, the Jew will forever struggle to come to terms with his identity. For many, as a recent Nazi war crimes trial in Jerusalem revealed, the Holocaust is the only thing that gives meaning to their Jewish identity! This is a sad reality that was lamented and yet recognised by many who wrote to the local press. It is as if many Jews are grappling to understand the deep feeling that they have about themselves. The truth is they feel Jewish but have no idea of what gives this feeling meaning or substance.

Secondly, their discovery of the simple and yet powerful Word of God will keep them from trying to be like all the other nations of the world. The Jew is different from all other peoples in that his origins go back to a special and super-natural act of God. This act was God's call to and friendship with Abraham (Genesis 12:1–3). This special relationship with Abraham was ratified by means of an eternal covenant (Genesis 17:1–8). Abraham's children's function in the world was, and is to be, the channel through which God would, and will, make His word known in the earth (Romans 9:4–5). Israel was therefore born to be a light to the nations (Isaiah 60:11–13).

Thus, the Jew has a special relationship to the Word of God, because in giving it birth it carved its indelible stamp upon him. As a result, he is different from other nations. They may receive the Word, but a Jew exists physically because of it! He may seek to deny this difference, as many do, but he will always feel it, just as a mother has a special link with a child that a father doesn't have, since the child came from within her. This is, no doubt, a mystery, but, as Paul said concerning another subject, I speak with reference to the Jew and the Word of God!

It is no secret that the testimony of thousands of Jews is that their Jewishness has more to do with their 'being' than with education or learning. A Jew will always feel his Jewishness even though he may seek to act and think like a Gentile. The God of heaven has made him so and a vital part of this making process was accomplished by the Word of God. A Jew therefore who comes alive to the Word of God, becomes a flaming torch of God's love in a way that no other can. The simple truth is this: the Word of God is best at home in a Jew. Just as a Ford engine functions best in a Ford car because the car was made for it!

Jesus recognised this truth and said that the Word of God was to first go to the house of Israel (Matthew 10:5–7). Its message of healing is the children's bread (Mark 7:27). That is, it belongs first and foremost to Israel.

In the light of all the above, imagine what will happen when this special nation again takes the Word of God to its heart. Have you ever considered the implications that this will have for the world? Well, God has promised that this will happen again! Ezekiel saw a day when the Word of God would again be breathed into the whole nation of Israel which had become desolate and barren, like dry bones

(Ezekiel 37:1–6). As a result they stood up as a mighty army – yea, a terrifying one and they were fully equipped with the Word of the Living God! (Ezekiel 37:7–11)

This will only happen if we who have been so blessed by their scriptures, repair the 'water gate' with fervent and persistent prayer. Let us do so 'For The World's Sake'.

8.   The 'Horse Gate'

'Above the Horse Gate the priests carried out repairs, each in front of his house.'   (Nehemiah 3:28 NASB)

In scripture the horse always speaks of war. It is an animal of war as history adequately declares. Jesus, scripture tells us, returns to earth riding on a horse, as He comes to make war with the nations.

'And I saw heaven opened; and behold, a white horse, and He Who sat upon it is called Faithful and True, and in righteousness He judges and wages war ...'
(Revelation 19:11 NASB)

The book of Job describes the horse as an animal that takes enthusiastically to the scent and noise of battle and fearlessly carries its rider into the thick of it (Job 39:19–25).

Israel has fought many hard battles. Her long history has been punctuated by wars. Some of these she has brought upon herself because of sin and disobedience. However, others have been initiated by the powers of darkness who have sought, by all means possible through the ages, to destroy her, since she holds the key to world redemption (Revelation 12:1–6). This has never changed! The devil is intent on her destruction today, as much as he ever was. Since the restoration of the modern state of Israel in 1948 she has had to fight a number of cruel wars in order to ensure her existence. Thus far she has survived – but only because of prayer.

Christians must understand that the physical survival of the Jewish people is crucial to God's plan of world redemption. For this reason Christians who embrace anti-Semitism are in league with the devil!

In view of the ever increasing antagonism and hatred against Israel, we are to pray as never before for her security and physical welfare. Israel is still surrounded by enemies on every side who would dearly love to see her destruction. Demonic deception will continue to stir up the nations against her and, finally, such deception will drive all nations to come down against her (Revelation 16:13–14). By the most terrifying weapons of war they will seek to annihilate her. Scripture declares that they will fail. Why? Because praying men and women have rebuilt the 'Horse Gate'.

Will you be amongst that praying number?

9. The 'East Gate'

'After Him Zadok, the son Immer carried out repairs in front of his house. And after him Shemaiah the son of Shechaniah, the keeper of the East Gate, carried out repairs ...'   (Nehemiah 3:29 NASB)

Our preceding chapters have shown that the 'East Gate' refers to the second coming of Jesus. We have also shown how important the restoration of Israel is to the return of Jesus to this world. The Bible teaches that Jesus's second coming can be hastened by the godly and dedicated behaviour of God's believing community on earth.

'Since all these things are to be destroyed in this way, what sort of people ought you to be in holy conduct and godliness, looking for and hastening the coming of the day of God ...'   (II Peter 3:11–12 NASB)

Without a doubt, prayer plays a vital role in the believer's life of dedication and in this sacred task of hastening the day of Jesus's return.

All prayer for Israel should therefore be exercised with the second coming of Jesus in mind. Indeed, all Christian activity should be discharged in the light of the second advent of Jesus. We are to constantly love the day of His appearing.

The flame of Israel will never be extinguished.

'In the future there is laid up for me the crown of righteousness, which the Lord, the Righteous Judge, will award to me on that day; and not only to me, but also to all who have loved His appearing ...'

(II Timothy 4:8 NASB)

Also, we are to be continuously looking towards it:

'For the grace of God has appeared bringing, salvation to all men, instructing us to deny ungodliness and worldly desires and to live sensibly, righteously and godly in the present age, looking for the blessed hope and the appearing of the glory of our great God and Saviour, Christ Jesus ...' (Titus 2:11–13 NASB)

It is important for us to remember that the second coming of Jesus not only ushers in a new day of peace and righteousness for the nations, but it will also elevate Israel to a place of glory and prominence amongst the nations. Speaking of Israel, the prophet Isaiah declares:

141

'And the nations will see your righteousness and all kings your glory; and you will be called by a new name, which the mouth of the Lord will designate. You will also be a crown of beauty in the hand of the Lord, and a royal diadem in the hand of your God ...'

(Isaiah 62:2–3 NASB)

So, then, the second coming of Jesus will usher in the day of Israel's exhaltation in the sight of the nations. It will be a day of indescribable joy in Israel, especially in view of the long dark tunnel of sorrow that she has endured through the successive ages of human history. Israel's promised glorious end should inspire us to pray for her regularly and specifically.

As we build the 'East Gate' of prayer, we shall find ourselves inspired and further encouraged to continue praying for her, even if our prayers for the moment seem to be making little impact on the world around us. Israel's glory will be the world's glory. We must pray for her, 'For The World's Sake!'

10. The 'Inspection Gate'

'After him, Malchijah, one of the goldsmiths, carried out repairs as far as the house of the temple servants and of the merchants, in front of the Inspection Gate and as far as the upper room of the corner ...'

(Nehemiah 3:31 NASB)

The 'Inspection' or 'Mustering Gate' speaks of completion or conclusion. There will certainly come a day when all of us will be mustered at God's great and glorious throne to be inspected. Paul wrote:

'But you, why do you judge your brother? Or you again, why do you regard your brother with contempt? For we shall all stand before the judgment seat of God ...'

(Romans 14:10 NASB)

This coming day of 'inspection' will determine the reward we each one will receive for faithfully serving Christ on earth

(I Corinthians 3:10–15). It will then not have anything to do with our salvation or entrance into God's eternal dwelling place; but it will seek to determine our lot or position in that place of glorious, eternal abode.

At the heart of all God's redemptive actions on earth through history, has been the Jewish people. Man's eternal salvation was and is the motivation for these actions. Even when God became a man in Jesus, he was born a Jew!

No wonder at the time of their formation as a people, God pronounced a blessing upon all those that would love, bless and comfort them.

> 'And I will bless those who bless you, and the one who curses you I will curse. And in you all the families of the earth shall be blessed ...' (Genesis 12:3 NASB)

Jesus Himself reinforced this in Matthew 25:45. Speaking of the nation of Israel, He said:

> '... Truly I say to you, to the extent that you did not do it to one of the least of these, you did not do it to me ...'

Crucial to our service for God is the question of our love and support for the Jewish nation. Those who recognise this truth are flowing with the very heart of God's purposes for the whole world.

Prayer – that is, talking to God regularly in the light of His Word, about this vital nation – is the most needful and important work that we can do! It will unleash untold redemptive blessings upon the nations of our world. It is also the area of greatest spiritual conflict since this ancient people are the springboard or foundation from which God initiated all His redemptive purposes in the earth.

The redemption story began with Israel and it will close with her. The devil knows this and does everything possible to prevent God's children from recognising it and doing something constructive about it! His most diabolical accomplishment has been to stir up the believing community in the world against the Jews. Anti-Semitism has been a sad and unfortunate part of the church's history! It is devil inspired and initiated. It also takes root in the heart of those who are far from the heart of God.

As Paul considered the importance of Israel to God's salvation plan, he wrote that his response was a prayerful one.

> 'Brethren, my heart's desire and **my prayer** to God for them is for their salvation ...'   (Romans 10:1)

Our response should be the same. I have no doubt that the coming day of 'inspection' will lavishly reward those who have laboured long and hard in prayer for that which has been the Creator's cornerstone in world redemption – namely; Israel.

Let us work while we still have opportunity and time and let us do so with the 'Inspection Gate' in view.

'For The World's Sake', pray for Israel!

Part Three

Eschatological and Historical

Foreword

It is always good to read a sound scriptural and theological book on the subject of Israel, especially since there are so many books and pamphlets that are shallow, unscriptural and self-seeking in this field.

Malcolm Hedding, the Chaplain of the International Christian Embassy, Jerusalem, and a devoted servant of the Lord, has written a book that will, for those who read it, guard them against all the unbiblical teachings that endeavour to influence Christians against God's ultimate plan and purpose with His people, Israel.

So important is this plan that Paul enters into a doxology of praise after he writes about it in his famous eleventh chapter of Romans.

So important that the Evil One, in his madness, is gathering all nations against Israel because he apparently takes what Paul writes about Israel's destiny more seriously than many in the Church do. He knows that while, 'their diminishing has been the riches of the Gentiles', their fullness will be none other than 'life from the dead'.

Therefore we hope that this book will be widely read and that wherever it goes it may carry the anointing of the God of Abraham, Isaac and Jacob, the God of Jesus Christ our Lord.

Jan Willem van der Hoeven
June 1988

Chapter 11

The gathering storm

'For behold, in those days and at that time, when I restore the fortunes of Judah and Jerusalem, I will gather all the nations and bring them down to the valley of Johoshaphat, and I will enter into judgment with them there, on account of my people and my heritage Israel ...' (Joel 3:1–2 RSV)

'Lo, I am about to make Jerusalem a cup of reeling to all the peoples round about; it will be against Judah also in the siege against Jerusalem. On that day I will make Jerusalem a heavy stone for all the peoples; all who lift it shall grievously hurt themselves. And all the nations of the earth will come together against it ...' (Zechariah 12:2–3 RSV)

The day of shaking

Scripture reveals that a day of shaking is coming:

> '... I am about to shake the heavens and the earth, and to overthrow the throne of kingdoms; I am about to destroy the strength of the kingdoms of the nations and overthrow the chariots and their riders ...'
>
> (Haggai 2:21–22 RSV)

The emergence of a restored Jewish State upon the world arena has shaken every conceivable man-made foundation.

A restored Israel – shaking the foundations of our world.

This is true of the secular humanistic world where God is generally denied, forgotten and ruled out of the affairs of men. Israel's restoration and preservation in the face of overwhelming obstacles and impossible odds has effectively shattered the myth of a dead God. Her on-going existence has no logical explanation save one that has to do with the covenant-keeping God of the Bible.

In the religious world a similar upheaval has taken, and is also now taking place. Christian theologians who have tenaciously propagated a 'Replacement Theology' which makes the Church everything and teaches that Israel is finished and no longer crucial to God's plan of world redemption, are now struggling to maintain their false teaching, since with every passing year biblical prophecy is more and more finding accurate fulfilment in the land of Israel.

The existence of Israel is constantly challenging these man-made doctrines that have infiltrated the Church throughout its history and which have played such a major role in fuelling the fires of anti-Semitism.

Fifty years ago when Israel was nothing more than a doubtful longing in the hearts of a handful of Jewish pioneers such teachings could still find a ready hearing and widespread acceptance in the Church. Now, however, their foundations have cracked and men and women everywhere are re-examining the prophetic word that shines like a burning lamp in a dark place (II Peter 1:19).

However, not only has the Christian world been challenged by the restoration of Israel but the Islamic world is also finding itself in an ever-increasing dilemma. This is so because the existence of a Jewish state in the heart of the Islamic region is unthinkable and impossible for the Muslim.

It is a type of spiritual nightmare, since Islam teaches that such a thing could never happen. According to the Koran, God is finished with Israel and with the Christians. They have apostasized and now Muhammed constitutes His last word to the world. Islam's credibility stands as long as these two religious groupings remain under its heel.

For this reason Jews and Christians are called 'Dhimmis' in the Koran, that is, second-class citizens always beneath

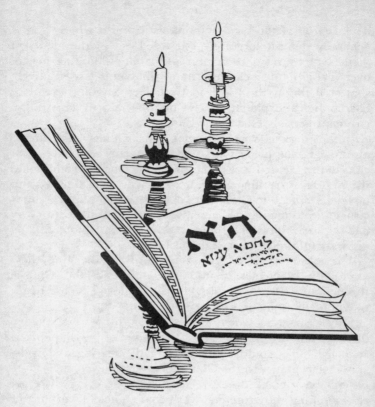

תורה

פרשת עקו

A flourishing Jewish state challenges the credibility of Isalm.

the dignity of a Muslim. It also explains why, to this present day, the Arab Islamic states have refused to speak directly to Israel and have maintained a state of war with her. Those Arab leaders who have talked with her, like Anwar Sadat of Egypt and Jemayel of Lebanon have been shot for so doing!

A thriving, victorious Jewish state therefore challenges the foundation upon which Islam stands. If God is finished with Israel – some 2,000 years ago – then how come He has allowed her re-emergence in the Islamic world?!!

The answer is simple; God is not finished with her and the true Word of God is not the Koran but the Hebrew Scriptures known as the Bible, and the true God of this world is

152

not the God of Islam but the God of Abraham, Isaac and Jacob.

A flourishing Jewish state constantly challenges the credibility of the Islamic revelation and therefore Israel's liquidation is not only desirable but an urgent necessity. This is the real issue behind the so-called Arab/Israeli conflict. It is the unseen agenda that makes this conflict religious and not political by nature.

Israel's unique position also challenges the stability of the world at large. The Arabs coupled with their oil wealth and their traditional links to the Soviet Union and Israel's military might coupled with her strong relationship with the United States of America makes the region an Armageddon scenario for the world. Yes, Israel challenges the very flimsy foundations of our world.

How true the Word of God is! It speaks of a day when God will shake everything that is not rooted in Him. This will be a world-shaking – nothing will escape!

> '... but now He has promised, yet once more I will shake not only the earth but also the heaven. This phrase, "Yet once more", indicates the removal of what is shaken, as of what has been made, in order that what cannot be shaken may remain ...' (Hebrews 12:26–27 RSV)

This shaking, according to the Hebrew prophets, has to do with a restored Jewish state. She is the catalyst. Her existence has world implications. Soon, yes very soon, all nations, in their wrath and anger against God will converge on the plains of Israel to do battle with her, with one another and with God Himself, Whom they have hated and Whose Word they have spurned.

> '... And I saw, issuing from the mouth of the dragon and from the mouth of the beast and from the mouth of the false prophet, three foul spirits like frogs, for they are demonic spirits, performing signs, who go abroad to the kings of the whole world to assemble them for battle on the great day of God the Almighty ... And they

assembled them at the place which is called in Hebrew
Armageddon ...'   (Revelation 16:13–16 RSV)

Sober reflection

When all is said and done, Israel speaks to the world about
God. Her restoration according to His Word is a sober
reminder to all that man has to answer to God in the final
analysis. Anti-Semitism is therefore anti-Godism. Not only
must Islam get rid of Israel in order to establish the
supremacy of its revelation but the world must also plot her
overthrow so as to vanquish the thought of God – the Judeo-
Christian ethic – from its collective conscience. Israel is a
'foreign body', she is not wanted in our world.

Throughout history every generation has had its own
group of Pharoahs, Hamans and Hitlers who have desired to
destroy her. The same is true today. Some evil mind is
always intent on her destruction or, at the very least, intent
on blaming the Jew for the troubles of our world.

Israel is aware of this demonic phenomenon and thus at a
gathering of world Jewish leaders in Jerusalem recently
Robert Maxwell from England said,

> 'The lessons of this century, of the holocaust, of the
> history of the Jewish people, are that peace and security
> cannot be assured by promises, by United Nations res-
> olutions, or by professions of good intent, whether they
> emanate from Washington, London, Moscow or wher-
> ever Yasser Arafat's caravan has rested. Israel requires
> deeds, not words. It does not need paper assurances. It
> needs guarantees made of steel. Since the civilized world
> cannot produce such guarantees, Israel must look after
> its own defence. In the final analysis, the only people the
> Jews can trust for their survival are the Jews
> themselves ...'

Another delegate at the same conference, Simon
Wiesenthal, expressed the same truth when he said,

> 'Over 40 years I was looking for justice ... I have seen
> that in times of danger, Jews are always alone ...'

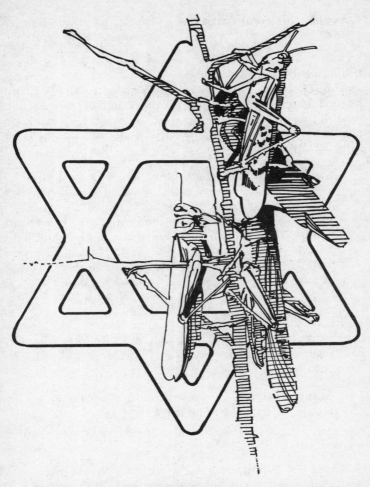

Every generation has its Pharoahs and Hamans who desire to liquidate Israel.

This persistent onslaught against Israel has a biblical answer. Israel has been the vehicle whereby God has chosen to bless our world with His redemptive truth. In other words through her God has shone His light and love into our world. For this reason the devil has opposed her since the very beginning of her creation (Revelation 12:1–4).

An eschatological reality

Israel's restoration is truly an eschatological event. That is, an event that has to do with the end of one age and with the beginning of another. The world is now in the 'terminal season'. Terminal, not in the sense of destruction without hope, but terminal in the sense that ungodliness, sin and death are about to be dealt a crushing blow by the soon coming Saviour who will come forth from heaven to fight for Israel and Jerusalem from the Mount of Olivet.

> '... For I will gather all the nations against Jerusalem to battle, and the city shall be taken and the houses plundered and the women ravished; half of the city shall go into exile, but the rest of the people shall not be cut off from the city. Then the Lord will go forth and fight against those nations as when He fights on a day of battle. On that day His feet will stand on the Mount of Olives which lies before Jerusalem on the east ...'
>
> (Zechariah 14:2–4 RSV)

His coming will usher in a new day of peace and righteousness since He alone is the Prince of Peace. The prophet Zechariah describes His rule of righteousness and peace in these terms,

> 'And the Lord will become King over all the earth; on that day the Lord will be one and His name one ...'
>
> (Zechariah 14:9 RSV)

Israel's restoration, survival and on-going existence is God's way of telling the world to prepare for the gathering storm. Since Jerusalem will be the epicentre of this storm it is not coincidental that she is more and more becoming the focus of world attention.

The question of Jerusalem is now discussed everywhere in the world's halls of government. One Arab politician recently stated that if the conflict over Jerusalem is not speedily resolved it has within it the potential to drag the whole world down into a dark abyss of destruction. The hour is exceedingly late and the fact that in Israel's 40th year a raging conflict, now known as the Palestinian uprising or Intifada, broke out within her borders; a conflict that rages ultimately over who has the right to govern from Jerusalem, is a further warning that our world is about to be judged by a holy God who is tired of sin, wickedness and rebellion. Yes, we have moved into the 'terminal season'.

Paul said that every true blood-washed believer would have the spiritual perception to understand these things:

> 'But as to the times and the seasons, brethren, you have no need to have anything written to you. For you yourselves know well that the day of the Lord will come like a thief in the night. When people say, 'there is peace and security', then sudden destruction will come upon them ...'   (I Thessalonians 5:1–3 RSV)

So then recognising the present battle for possession of Jerusalem and given the strategic alliances that both sides in this conflict enjoy, it is easy to perceive that in the next few years the battle for Jerusalem will only intensify. Ultimately, as Scripture predicts, all nations will be swept into this raging storm. Only the appearing of the Lord Jesus will bring this conflict to an end. This is the only hope of our world.

Over the last few years there has been an escalation in talks about peace and security. In most cases 'peace', so called, has come at great cost; namely, the enslavement of the masses to the ungodly forces of religious fundamentalism and Marxist Communism. This is not peace! It is satanic bondage. It will yet drive all of humanity into a one-world order over which a demonic personage endowed with super-natural powers will preside. This is the clear warning of Scripture!

> 'Let no one deceive you in any way; for that day will not come, unless the rebellion comes first, and the man of lawlessness is revealed, the son of perdition, who opposes and exalts himself against every so-called God or object of worship, so that he takes his seat in the temple of God, proclaiming himself to be God ... and then that lawless

one will be revealed, and the Lord Jesus will slay him with the breath of his mouth and destroy him by his appearing and his coming. The coming of the lawless one by the activity of satan will be with all power and with pretended signs and wonders and with all wicked deception for those who are to perish, because they refused to love the truth and so be saved ...'

(II Thessalonians 2:3–4, 8–10 RSV)

A day of decision

The above scenario is rapidly unfolding before our eyes. World leaders are now calling more and more for the implementation of a world government. Globalism is everywhere being debated and major environmental issues such as the destruction of the ozone layer and the rain forests of Brazil are being highlighted as reasons why the world should become a 'global village'.

The same momentum is discernible in the religious world. The Pope is travelling the globe and forging religious alliances with every conceivable religious movement. In 1986 he convened a world peace prayer conference that included Muslims, Hindus, Buddhists, snake worshippers, Jews and Christians ... and others. Even charismatics are now forging greater unity with Rome and talking of global Christianity. The essentials of our faith are being surrendered on every side and soon the Bible-believing, born-again Christian who refuses to be a part of this watered down all-embracing Christian religious system will be considered dangerous and obstructive to the new world-governing religious order. A day of persecution is coming. John saw it and spoke of it in these terms:

'And the beast was given a mouth uttering haughty and blasphemous words ... Also it was allowed to make war on the saints and to conquer them. And authority was given it over every tribe and people and tongue and nation, and all who dwell on earth will worship it ...'

(Revelation 13:5, 7–8 RSV)

God's purposes with Israel have been clear for all to see.

Now, more than ever the Church must make up her mind as to where she will stand. This is not an irrelevant matter. Apostasy is a deceptive process and it doesn't happen over night.

For decades, God has been warning His people about these things. Moreover, His purposes with Israel have been clear and highly visible for all in the household of God to see. Israel is His doorway into the world. Her restoration, preservation and recapturing of Jerusalem will therefore be opposed by demonic forces everywhere. Increasingly Israel, like the true blood-washed born-again believers, will be castigated as the 'bad boy' in the world arena. To stand with her will be exceedingly unpopular and yet the visible second coming of Jesus will be dependent upon her survival and spiritual restoration.

God expects His people to have grasped these basic-truths by now. A gathering storm is coming and it saddens me to see that many in the born-again, evangelical, charismatic church are allying themselves with the forces of darkness against Israel. They are presently being blinded by doctrines of excessive Christian triumphalism.

The new theologies

For them, Jesus is not returning to the world when Israel invites Him back in her hour of greatest need (Matthew 23:37–39) but rather, He is returning only after the Church has literally conquered all the nations of the world and subjected them to her governing authority. The Church, we are now being told, will establish the millenium and then, having subdued the nations, invite Jesus to come back and take control.

These are the deceptive teachings now being propagated everywhere by those who call themselves Reconstructionists, Kingdom Now believers and Dominionists. In reality this is nothing short of apostasy. These deluded false teachers are about to push the Church into the arms of the coming antichrist, who as we have seen, has a similar religious programme for world government.

The New Age Movement

Moreover, these so called 'Kingdom Now' or 'New Triumphalist' teachers are advocating spiritual techniques that are looking increasingly like the 'spiritual techniques' of the New Age Movement. In this regard I am referring to their emphasis upon mind realisation, positive thinking and 'particular vocabulary' or positive confession. Confession of sin or failure is not encouraged since these are negative!! The whole thing smacks of Eastern religion, which, by the way, is the underlying spiritual influence behind the New Age Movement, and which lays emphasis upon the fact that we are an integral part of God, we are therefore God, and all we need to do is recognise our true identity and potential. When people in sufficient numbers come to this realisation, our world, according to New Agers, will take a quantum leap into a new age. An age, we are told, that will free humanity from its present troubles. Christian, be warned!

The restoration of Israel, according to God's prophetic Word has more to do with our spiritual health and survival than we think.

For years I have listened to preachers telling me that we should not get too involved with this 'Israel thing'. This, in spite of the fact that prophetic teaching or eschatology relating to her constitutes the major doctrinal thesis of the Bible.

These preachers have ignored her, they have considered believers involved with her to be 'off the wall' but now these same preachers are 'buying' the false teachings of the Reconstructionists and Dominionists 'lock, stock and barrel'.

Their failure to appreciate the importance of Jerusalem in this last hour is leading them down the 'garden path' to Rome and its religious syncretism! You say impossible and somewhat exaggerated! Then why is it that in 1990 some of the biggest names in the evangelical Charismatic Movement are planning on travelling to Rome to award the Pope a so-called 'Prince of Peace Award'? Such a title is only reserved for Jesus in Scripture (Isaiah 9:6). Or, has the Charismatic Movement now recognised the Pope's claim to be the vicar of Christ on earth?

Undoubtedly these leaders are taking themselves and their trusting congregations into the strong delusion of the new world religious order. All in the name of Christian victory.

Agreement with the world

Yes, there is a gathering storm and the conflict over Jerusalem and the land of Israel is polarising the world and the Church. We are being forced to take sides. The day of spiritual decision has suddenly dawned upon us. Are we going to agree with God's eternal Word or are we going to flow with the pressure of the world?

We should be highly sceptical of Christian leaders who, in their teachings on Israel, side with the world, the United Nations and all the anti-God agencies of our world.

The Bible teaches that our world lies under the control of the devil:

> 'We know that we are of God, and the whole world is in the power of the evil one'.　　　　　　　　　(I John 5:19)

Moreover, Satan is described as that 'being' of darkness and evil that blinds the minds of the unbelievers from understanding the truth of Scripture.

> '... The god of this world has blinded the minds of the unbelievers, to keep them from seeing the light of the gospel of the glory of Christ, who is the likeness of God ...'　　　　　　　　　(II Corinthians 4:4 RSV)

A church then, that easily harmonises its teaching on Israel with that of the world is surely deceived!! In this connection I recently heard a well known American Charismatic preacher tell a big congregation in Durban, South Africa, that he and others have decided to henceforth undermine Israel's special relationship with the United States by using the strong influence of the born-again lobbying movement on the Bush administration in Washington.

How interesting this is, since Yasser Arafat is presently doing his utmost to achieve the same end! So Christian leaders are now actively supporting the same objectives that the P.L.O. has. This despite the fact that the P.L.O. is an organisation that has spilt innocent blood all over the world and which has proven links with every major terror group on the face of the globe.

This Christian leader, not surprisingly, is an outspoken Dominionist or Kingdom Now advocate!

God's voice to the world

Without a doubt the existence of Israel is God's way of telling us that a gathering storm is in the making. We are at the end. Jesus is coming and God's ancient people, the Jews, who have given so much blessing to our world will be redeemed and will yet give the world rest from its sorrows, violence, terror and wars by the coming of their King.

For Jesus is the King of the Jews and when He comes again He will cause them to dwell safely and securely in the land of their fathers. A land eternally bequeathed to them through Abraham their father.

In that day the Word of God will go forth from Jerusalem to the four corners of the earth and men will take their weapons of war and destruction and beat them into implements of peace and prosperity. Mankind will learn war no more and the nations will come to Jerusalem, that is, Jewish Jerusalem, year by year to celebrate the Feast of Tabernacles (Isaiah 2:1–4; Zechariah 14:16–19).

Swords will yet be beaten into instruments of agriculture.

The guarantee of a new day

The restoration of Israel is thus more than just a sign of forboding armageddon. She is more than a means by which God shakes the religious and secular foundations of our world. She is, in fact, the guarantee of a new day of blessing and joy for the whole world. God has promised to sanctify His name in all the earth, by the miracle of her survival in the face of insurmountable difficulties and odds.

> 'Thus says the Lord God, "Are you the one of whom I spoke in former days through My servants the prophets of Israel, who prophesied in those days for many years that I would bring you against them? And it will come about on that day when Gog comes against the land of Israel," declares the Lord God, "that My fury will mount up in My anger. And in My zeal and in My blazing wrath I declare that on that day there will surely be a great earthquake in the land of Israel. And the fish of the sea, the birds of the heavens, the beasts of the field, all the creeping things that creep on the earth, and all the men who are on the face of the earth will shake at My presence; the mountains also will collapse, and every wall will fall to the ground. And I shall call for a sword against him on all My mountains," declares the Lord God, "Every man's sword will be against his brother. And with pestilence and with blood I shall enter into judgment with him; and I shall rain on him, and on his troops, and on the many peoples who are with him, a torrential rain, with hailstones, fire, and brimstone. And I shall magnify Myself, sanctify Myself, and make Myself known in the sight of many nations; and they will know that I am the Lord."'
> (Ezekiel 38:17–23 NASB)

Our charge

Our responsibility to understand and teach these things is therefore great, since only sound biblical teaching on Israel will help keep the church from participating, albeit unwittingly, in an anti-God world order.

Moreover, every local church should be living out the biblical command to pray for the peace of Jerusalem (Psalm 122:6, Isaiah 62:6–7).

Understanding Israel is in the final analysis understanding your place in a world that is plunging toward judgment, Armageddon and blessing. Understanding Israel will help us prepare for and face the world-wide shaking that is beginning to make its presence felt in every corner of the globe. Understanding Israel is understanding the story of world redemption.

Chapter 12

Uprising

'Behold, I Myself have created the smith who blows the fire of coals, and brings out a weapon for its work; and I have created the destroyer to ruin. "No weapon that is formed against you shall prosper; and every tongue that accuses you in judgement you will condemn. This is the heritage of the servants of the LORD, and their vindication is from Me," declares the LORD.'

(Isaiah 54:16–17 NASB)

Media exploitation

The world media has recently exploited the so-called 'Intifada' or 'Palestinian Uprising' in a way that portrays Israel as a ruthless oppressor of the Palestinian people. Gullible journalists, anti-Semites and people in general, have unquestionably accepted the version of this sad episode emotively displayed on their television sets night after night.

Even while thousands were dying elsewhere in the world, in worse and more ruthless regional conflicts, Israel still remained, and remains, the number one issue. This in spite of the fact that only 350 people have died in the Gaza Strip and West Bank so far, over a period of one and a half years.

Naturally, that one person should die in any conflict anywhere in the world is in itself totally unacceptable and regrettable. However, when a million people die in

The whole world is against Jerusalem.

Afghanistan, thanks to Russian aggression, the world in no way campaigns against Moscow as it does now against Jerusalem. In fact, this Russian outrage did not even enjoy the specific condemnation of the United Nations. Oh yes, a resolution voicing regret at the invasion of that country was passed but it did not refer specifically to the Soviet Union.

This story can be repeated many times over, as many regional conflicts have raged in our world over the past two years, claiming far more lives than that of the 'Intifada'. In this regard, we need only think of the Middle Americas, Lebanon, the Persian Gulf, the Punjab Province of India and Sri Lanka ... to name but a few. However, in spite of all this, Israel remains the 'whipping boy' of the world media. More disturbing still is the fact that even the Christian media has climbed on the bandwagon of castigating Israel.

Naturally, most of the footage screened on television and the details written about the Palestinian Uprising ignore the historical facts behind the 'Intifada' and concentrate on the heart-rending tragedies of those who are being killed, injured and dispossessed by the conflict. Since the stone throwers are mostly teenagers, very intent on killing, by the way, the nightly broadcasts of scenes portraying Israeli soldiers fully armed and acting against them arouses antagonism and outrage against Israel. This constant portrayal of the supposedly innocent being oppressed by the overwhelmingly strong blurs truth, blunts the ability to react sensibly and stirs up hatred against the Jews everywhere.

Quite obviously this is intentional! There can be no other logical answer to the phenomenon. So quick is the world to condemn Israel that many cartoonists and writers have had the arrogance and downright ignorance to equate the events presently transpiring in the West Bank with the Holocaust! It seems that the world must, at all costs, blame the Jew for some atrocity so as to ease its own conscience over the murder of six million during the last war.

It is as if the world is trying to say, 'you are as bad as we are'. By the way, the world is responsible, with the Nazis, for the Holocaust. Before the war a special conference was called, which was attended by all the major western countries and others, to discuss the fate of the Jewish people in Europe. This conference, held in Evian Les Bains, in France, closed with all the nations refusing to give refuge to the Jewish people. Hitler was then told afterwards, by his leadership, that he could do what he liked with the Jews ... and he did!

In 1982, a similar attempt to discredit Israel, in a massive way, was perpetrated by the western media over the Lebanon affair. Again, the charge of 'Holocaust' was levelled against Israel over the massacre in the refugee camps of Sabra and Shatilla, committed, not by the Israelis, but by the South Lebanese Christian Militia. The western media eventually owned up to their duplicity in this matter, and even conceded that they were blackmailed, by the PLO, on the threat of death, to discredit Israel.

For instance, in his excellent book 'Now the Story Can Be Told', Eli Eyal writes:

> 'Intimidation of the foreign press was directed at those who presented the PLO in a negative light. One example was the German television network, ZDF, which was threatened by the PLO terror in Lebanon ...'

Again, Eyal writes that another French journalist, Edouard George, is

> 'compiling a history of the PLO intimidation of the press, both local and foreign. Between 1976 and 1981, he told Ma'Ariv on August 27, 1982, the PLO killed seven foreign journalists in West Beirut ...'

The intimidation and killing continued throughout this period and as a result, the world was given a distorted view of what was really going on. It may be worth noting here that a few years later, in 1985, a worse massacre took place in Sabra and Shatilla, resulting in the death of 500 people. This massacre of the Palestinians was perpetrated by Lebanese Arab Shi'ite forces and the world said nothing and probably still doesn't even know that it happened!

The point we are making in all this is that there is definitely a deliberate attempt by the world media to falsify facts and keep the truth from getting out when it involves Israel.

Eliyahu Tal, in his excellent work, 'Israel in Medialand' writes:

> 'The impression one gains is that the communications media pay rather less attention to violence and bloodshed occurring strictly within Arab ranks than they do to Middle East strife that involves Israelis too ...'

Yes, there is a conspiracy against Israel and as Christian people, we should wake up to this fact. The Palestinian uprising is another attempt by the forces of darkness to liquidate Israel. About this, we should have no illusions.

Moreover, people buy half-truths simply because they are not aware of the whole truth. That is, the historical facts that have shaped the present problems in Israel. Indeed, the average person today is not really interested in knowing all the facts. He believes the media and relies upon it for his instruction about world affairs and general knowledge. The media bosses are well aware of this and thus they know that the masses can be moved by the skillful manipulation of video material.

Ulla Järvilehto writes:

'A short survey of the historical facts tells us clearly that Israel has shown her willingness for peace and peaceful co-existence with her Arab neighbours repeatedly and convincingly ...'

So, what are the facts on the ground? Is there a story about the Palestinian uprising that is not being told? Yes there is! It begins in 1946.

Two Palestinian states

In that year England, the mandatory power in the Middle East, created a Palestinian state on the East Bank of the Jordan River called Transjordan. Today we know this state as Jordan. However, what people do not know is that it incorporated 77% of historical Palestine and thus over 70% of the

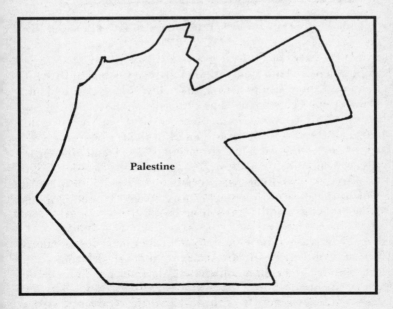

Palestine under England, the mandatory power until 1948.

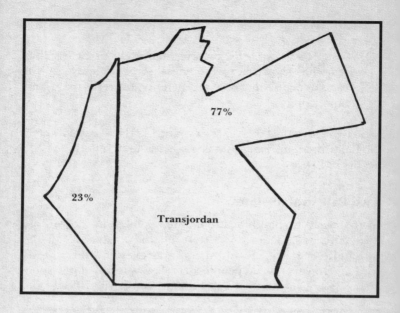

77%

23%

Transjordan

Palestine divided by England in 1946 thus creating the Palestinian state of Transjordan.

population are Palestinians making King Hussein, of Bedouin descent, a minority dictator. His army is in fact a Bedouin army and in years past he has ruthlessly subdued the Palestinians in his country. In September 1970, for instance, he expelled the PLO from Jordan and in the process murdered 15,000 Palestinians! This atrocity has been remembered as 'Black September'. However, to speak of the people of that country as Jordanians is incorrect. They are Palestinians! This is the clear testimony of history. Moshe Aumann, in his book 'The Palestinian Labyrinth' writes:

> 'The Hashemite Kingdom of Jordan meant the realisation of the Palestinian Arab's right of self-determination in more than three-fourths of Palestine ...'

Nevertheless, in spite of the fact that the Arabs now had a Palestinian state – indeed between 1948 and 1967 some

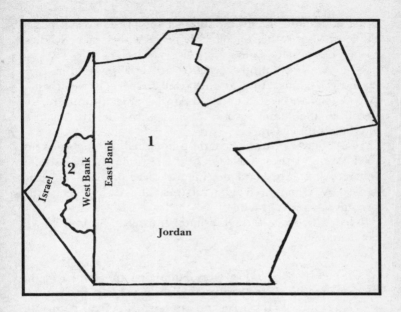

Palestine re-divided by UN partition plan of 1947 thereby creating Israel and a second Palestinian state.

400,000 Palestinians in the West Bank moved to Jordan on the East Bank – the United Nations agreed in 1948 to further partition West Bank Palestine into two states, thus creating Israel and a second Palestinian state! This second Palestinian state would incorporate Judea and Samaria now known as the West Bank ... and after the successful implementation of the partition plan, either join with Jordan, join with Israel or become linked to both.

Remarkably the Jewish leadership of the day accepted this second Palestinian state plan and immediately stated their desire to live at peace with their Arab neighbours. The Arabs on the other hand, rejected the proposal and immediately mobilised for a war of liquidation.

So within hours of the establishment of the State of Israel, on May 14, 1948, the fledgling state found itself facing the collective fire power of five Arab armies. In fact, Golda Meir had undertaken a very dangerous trip to Jordan so as to ask

King Abdallah, the grandfather of the present king, not to make war but rather to conclude peace with Israel. Needless to say, her mission failed.

The Arabs promptly expelled 800,000 Jews from their countries, confiscating at the same time their wealth and possessions and called upon all Arabs living within Israel to flee from their homes so as to escape the destruction that would fall upon Israel.

In all, 600,000 Arabs fled, despite Israel's urging them not to do so, and these 600,000 Arabs became the Palestinian refugees of today. The Palestinian refugee problem was thus caused by Arab hatred against Israel. The Arabs, even to this present day, acknowledge this!

Khaled El-Azm, former Prime Minister of Syria writes in his memoirs:

'Since 1948 it is we who demanded the return of the refugees to their country, while it is we who made them leave it ... Is this wise and established policy? Is this the coordination in planning? We brought disaster upon one million Arab refugees, by inviting them and bringing pressure to bear upon them, to leave their land, their homes, their work and their industry. We have rendered them dispossessed, unemployed, whilst everyone of them had work or a trade by which he could gain his livelihood ... We exploited them in executing crimes of murder, arson, and throwing bombs upon houses and vehicles carrying men, women, and children – all this in the service of political purposes in Lebanon and Jordan ...'

By the time the War of Independence ended in 1948, the Arab armies had been defeated but the Arabs had gained control of the West Bank, Gaza and East Jerusalem.

Jordan promptly and illegally annexed the West Bank – the world said nothing – and them together with Egypt and Lebanon, allowed their Palestinian brethren to languish in the most appalling conditions for the next 19 years in refugee camps.

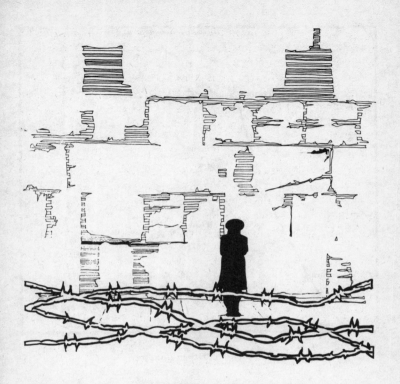

In 1948 Israel lost the West Bank to Jordan including East or Old Jerusalem.

In 1964, when the Arabs still held, in terms of the West Bank, everything that they say they want today, the PLO was formed with the express purpose, still enshrined in its charter, of the destruction of Israel, that is all of Israel.

A major strategy in this conquest plan was the manipulation of the Palestinian peoples. The Arabs quickly recognised that a people left indefinitely in squalid conditions would become a real threat to Israel.

The situation deteriorated and the Arabs, still sufficiently confident of a military victory, made rapid preparations for another showdown with Israel on the field of battle. Egypt became Israel's main antagonist and as the signs of impending war became more obvious, Israel urged Jordan, which as we

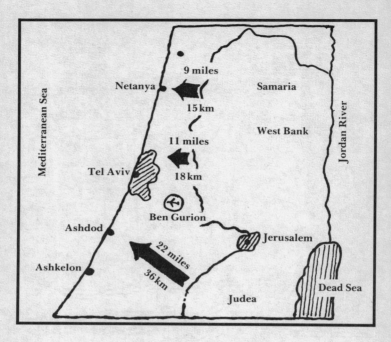

Israel's security nightmare.

have noted controlled the West Bank and East Jerusalem, not to enter the war. Israel promised Jordan that she would not attack her. On the 6th of June 1967, hostilities broke out and Israel found herself in another life and death struggle for survival. Initially, Jordan stayed out of the war but when Nasser, of Egypt, recognised that he was about to be defeated, he contacted King Hussein of Jordan, falsified the facts by speaking of imminent Arab victory and urged him to enter the war.

Hussein, not wanting to appear as the coward in the light of an impending Arab victory, attacked Israel and promptly lost East Jerusalem and the West Bank. The rest is history.

That which is not too well known is the fact that Israel immediately offered to return the West Bank to Jordan on the condition that the Arabs negotiate a permanent and lasting peace with her. The offer was flatly rejected and a state of war with Israel has existed ever since. Indeed, the official Arab response was, 'No peace with Israel, no negotiations with Israel and no recognition of Israel ...'

This rejection of peace left Israel with no other recourse than to hold the so-called 'Occupied Territories' so as to ensure her security. The much-disputed Jewish settlement programme became and is, a major foundation stone of Israel's security policy. For instance, Jerusalem is now surrounded on every side with new settlements, thus no longer making her vulnerable to attack. This is a type of buffer strategy which in the light of repeated Arab intransigence is perfectly understandable.

The Arabs, in their determination to annihilate Israel, have missed one opportunity after another to get what they say they want today. They have rejected every peace offer by Israel and have used their fabulous oil wealth to manipulate world opinion into believing that Israel is the 'bad boy' in the Middle East peace process.

Ulla Järvilehto writes:

> 'When we look at Israel in the light of historical facts, we don't find an aggressive attacker, but we do find a little democratic judicial state and a persevering nation, which bravely holds on to her existence and independence, and strives in every way possible towards peace with her neighbours so as to build her country and bring up her children in safety ...'

On the other hand, Egypt, the only Arab nation thus far prepared to talk about peace directly with Israel, has found that such talks have delivered the goods. The rest of the Arab world continues to seek third parties, notably the PLO, by which to pursue their relentless strategy of Israel's liquidation.

And what of the PLO? No other terror group upon the face of this earth has spilt innocent blood like this organisation has. Countless thousands have died, most of them innocently, as they have spread their reign of terror from the Middle East to nearly every part of the globe.

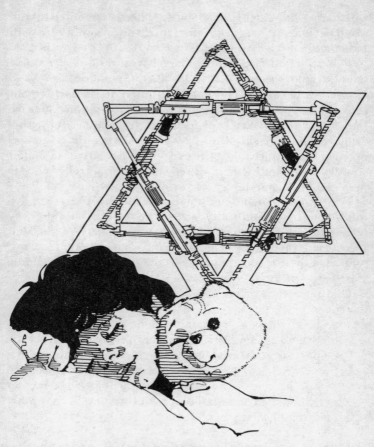

Israel wants to bring up her children in safety.

Millions of Arab oil dollars have been pumped into the PLO, dollars that would have many times over relieved the poverty and hardship of the very people they claim to represent.

Israel, recognising the need to solve this human tragedy of a people caught in a 'no mans land' as it were, has repeatedly offered the Palestinians total autonomy over their affairs, except that of defence – for obvious reasons. In fact, the Camp

David Accords made explicit provision for such an arrangement.

However, due to Arab pressure and intimidation from the PLO, such a plan has been rejected out of hand. It is a dead option because the goal in this conflict is not the welfare of the Palestinian people but rather the liquidation of the Jewish state. Thus, a stalemate has a long time ago been reached, leaving the future of the Palestinians looking decidedly dismal.

Since this unhappy business began in 1948, a generation of embittered Palestinians have grown up without any hope. As Israel constitutes the only authority structure they immediately relate to, she has become the obvious target of their bitterness. In a sense, one can understand this and as Christian people, we can only relate to this story of human suffering with compassion, prayerfulness and constructive action. However, the picture of this sad story becomes grossly distorted if we do not know the true facts behind it. The Bible says that Christian love is not just compassion or even constructive action. No, it also constitutes rejoicing in the truth!

> 'Love is patient, love is kind and is not jealous; love does not brag and is not arrogant, does not act unbecomingly; it does not seek its own, is not provoked, does not take into account a wrong suffered, does not rejoice in unrighteousness, *but rejoices with the truth*; bears all things, believes all things, hopes all things, endures all things, love never fails ...'   (I Corinthians 13:4–8 NASB)

In my experience, many Christians have been so heavily influenced by the media that they don't want to know the truth behind the Palestinian uprising. In this context, they repeatedly fling moral salvos at one like, 'don't you care about justice and suffering?' or 'are you trying to suggest that Israel has never done anything wrong?' For them, truth means nothing and all that matters are principles of morality. It all sounds very Christian but if we do not couple our sense of morality with truth, we shall end up supporting the goals of evil men. The present-day marriage between Liberation Theology and

179

Marxism is but one example of this. Principles of freedom and justice are said to be the reason for such an unholy marriage. However, the outcome is always the total removal of such virtues. The magazine 'Family Protection Scoreboard' comments:

'Liberation Theology's lack of interest in political freedom is apparent in its almost total silence about totalitarianism in Eastern Europe. After all, people in Eastern Europe are also oppressed and poor. Should not the Liberation theologians say something on their behalf?

Why, for example, are they so silent about oppressed Jews in the Soviet Union or suffering Christians in Poland? People who claim to be concerned about justice and freedom should condemn bondage wherever it exists, even in the Marxist states of the world. Ironically, there is a modest revolution beginning in Eastern Europe; but it is a revolution against Marxism. Perhaps that is why Marxist-oriented liberationists say nothing about it.'

Again, 'Scoreboard' writes:

'Christian opponents of Liberation Theology do not dispute the Christian's obligation to care for the poor and to alleviate oppression. What they dispute is the agenda by which liberation thinkers insist this duty must be fulfilled.'

Quite obviously a conflict such as the Palestinian one violates many virtues of human behaviour and justice clearly lies trampled upon in the streets. Israel has made many mistakes and lives are at times wasted in the fury of anger. However, truth is still truth and it had better be made known.

The PLO has now claimed to recognise Israel's right to exist. Such a declaration was made on the 15th of November 1988. To mark the occasion, the PLO issued a so-called 'birth certificate', which was subsequently published in the Persian Gulf newspapers in February 1989. Strangely, the emblem on this PLO birth certificate shows the new state of Palestine as stretching from the Mediterranean to the Jordan River. Israel is nowhere to be seen!

Since Yasser Arafat's bold declaration, world leaders have been falling over themselves in order to get an audience with him. This despite the fact that the PLO Charter, which gives the PLO its charge, still calls for the liquidation of the Jewish state.

Moreover, major factions within the PLO have already branded Arafat a traitor and have distanced themselves from him; at the same time, vowing to continue the war of liquidation against Israel, no matter what. Already these groups are playing a major role in the Intifada and Arafat's ability to influence events on the ground is very doubtful. This has been proven as over the last few months, in spite of the PLO's undertaking to cease acts of terror against Israel, there has been an escalation in attempted infiltrations into Israel by PLO terror squads! One such infiltration took place on the Israel-Jordan border near the Dead Sea. This was unprecedented as this border has been quiet for years.

Tragically, over 300 people have died in this conflict and yet a short while after the PLO's declaration to recognise Israel's right to exist and to cease from acts of terror against her, a Pan Am jumbo jet, carrying 270 passengers – all of them innocent and uninvolved in the Intifada – was blown out of the sky over Scotland. Two hundred and seventy people died in one act of terror! Who perpetrated this atrocity? The B.B.C. said that the suspect(s) had been identified as a Palestinian who had gone into hiding and would shortly be arrested. You can be sure that the PLO was involved, in some way, in this crime. Naturally, the world will not have too much to say and the matter will pass with the usual political rhetoric that amounts to precious little. However, if the Israelis had been involved, you can be sure that the world would still be crying out 'Holocaust!!'. The media would have relentlessly hammered away at Israel night after night, and anti-Semitic cartoons would have appeared in every major western newspaper.

Sadly, truth has fallen in the streets. The devil, as of old, has found another group of Pharaohs by which to persecute (the woman) Israel and thus by doing so, attempt to destroy her.

'And when the dragon saw that he was thrown down to the earth, he persecuted the woman who gave birth to the male child. And the two wings of the great eagle were given to the woman, in order that she might fly into the wilderness to her place, where she was nourished for a time and times and half a time, from the presence of the serpent. And the serpent poured water like a river out of his mouth after the woman, so that he might cause her to be swept away with the flood. And the earth helped the woman, and the earth opened its mouth and drank up the river which the dragon poured out of his mouth. And the dragon was enraged with the woman, and went off to make war with the rest of her offspring, who keep the commandments of God and hold to the testimony of Jesus.'   (Revelation 12:13–17 NASB)

In the long run, Israel will stand all alone. The world will rage against her since they have failed to understand her. In that hour, the God of Israel will stand with her and according to Scripture, He will arise to pulverise her enemies.

'Behold, a day is coming for the Lord when the spoil taken from you will be divided among you. For I will gather all the nations against Jerusalem to battle, and the city will be captured, the houses plundered, the women ravished, and half of the city exiled, but the rest of the people will not be cut off from the city. Then the Lord will go forth and fight against those nations, as when He fights on a day of battle. And in that day His feet will stand on the Mount of Olives, which is in front of Jerusalem on the east ...'   (Zechariah 14:1–4 NASB)

Christians by all means love justice and righteousness and be filled with compassion but make sure you build these virtues upon truth, lest you be found ignorant and wanting!!

Neglect of the truth is a highway to darkness. This is the lasting message of the Reformation. Religious ideals are good but if they ignore truth, they become nothing more than the misguided deeds of the deceived. They will not further the

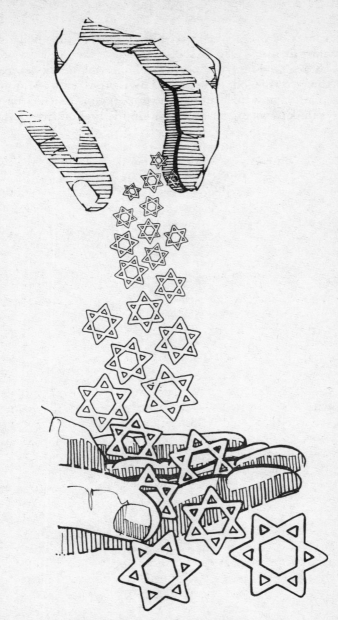

The God who birthed Israel will by His own hand preserve her.

purposes of God for our generation, indeed, they will work against them.

Understanding Israel begins with understanding her place in the Word of God. Jesus said, 'Thy Word is truth'. May God help us to know this truth and to forever cling to it, no matter how unpopular this may make us in the eyes of the world.